Ian I. Mitroff

Ralph H. Kilmann

Methodological Approaches to Social Science

 Jossey-Bass Publishers

San Francisco • Washington • London • 1978

METHODOLOGICAL APPROACHES TO SOCIAL SCIENCE
Integrating Divergent Concepts and Theories
  by Ian I. Mitroff and Ralph H. Kilmann

Copyright © 1978 by: Jossey-Bass, Inc., Publishers
                     433 California Street
                     San Francisco, California 94104
                                &
                     Jossey-Bass Limited
                     28 Banner Street
                     London EC1Y 8QE

Library of Congress Catalogue Card Number LC 78-62565

International Standard Book Number ISBN 0-87589-386-4

Manufactured in the United States of America

JACKET DESIGN BY WILLI BAUM

FIRST EDITION

Code 7826

The Jossey-Bass Social and
Behavioral Science Series

Preface

The tension between different views of science and scientific method in Western culture has reached the point at which it can no longer be ignored. When fundamental differences in attitude persist so long, and with such intensity, not only should we take them seriously but we should regard them as surface symptoms of a deeper phenomenon. *Methodological Approaches to Social Science* contends that the tension is symptomatic of basic psychological differences between the proponents of differing views of science. The purpose of this book is to examine—systematically and in depth—some of the underlying psychological and sociological reasons for the differing attitudes toward science. If an integrated methodology of science is ever to be achieved, it will only be through explicit and conscious understanding of the reasons that have brought about the divergence in views.

This book is one of a small but growing series of efforts in the social sciences and shares many features with earlier efforts. Most of all, it attempts to add unity to the methods and the knowledge of the social sciences. It also attempts to be intensely self-critical and self-reflective—both of these attitudes are considered vital in attaining unity of purpose, methods, and knowledge.

The points on which this book diverges from previous efforts are significant. It describes the differences in logic, style, and temperament of several fundamentally different ways of perceiving and conducting social science inquiries. However, unlike previous efforts—such as Paul Diesing's *Patterns of Discovery in the Social Sciences* (1971), which is strongly recommended as companion reading to the present volume—this book is not merely concerned with representing older, clearly established styles of inquiry but goes on to capture the spirit of newly emerging and not yet fully formed patterns of inquiry. It also differs in its attempt to account for various styles across the social sciences taken as a whole, as contrasted to a study such as George Ritzer's (1975), which is confined to differences that manifest themselves only within the field of sociology.

This book is not merely interdisciplinary, but *transdisciplinary*—it goes beyond the limitations and confines of disciplines as we currently conceive of them because the differences in which we are interested cut across more than one science. Our task demands that we be free to range across all of the social sciences. This does not mean that we will explicitly discuss the differences in all of the social sciences. However, we are well aware that our work is indebted to all of the social sciences even though we may not clearly acknowledge each and every one of them.

Another distinguishing feature of this book is its attempt to carry the notion of dialectics deeper into the concept of scientific methodology. Indeed, we contend that if dialectical reasoning is to have the impact on science that it deserves, the impact must occur on the level of the day-to-day activities of working scientists. To talk about dialectics merely in abstract terms not only misses one of the most vital aspects of dialectical reasoning—the fundamental tension and mutual interaction between conceptual and pragmatic aspects of scientific thought—but actually perpetuates the divergence between different views of science.

We have deliberately included some rather long quotations throughout the book in order to illustrate the differences we are talking about. In an admittedly speculative work such as this, such quotes help the reader understand our interpretation of the various views being discussed.

We have limited our analysis to four different views of science, which we feel sufficiently encompass the tension and divergence that currently exist. In characterizing each view we have also limited our discussion. Our purpose is not to give a detailed history of the development of each view and its literature but to present selective works, which illustrate the spirit of each tradition we are trying to describe. We offer a detailed account of what it is like to think in accordance with the dictates of each position and what it is like to practice it. An earlier version of Chapter Seven was published under the title of "Systemic Knowledge: Toward an Integrated Theory of Science" (*Theory and Society*, 1977, *4* (1), 101–128).

The people instrumental in writing this book are too numerous for us to list, but they know who they are and how much we have enjoyed their company and help. However, we would like to acknowledge our mentors, who more than anyone else set us on the present path. They sensitized us to the notions and taught us not only how personal science is but how to practice it and revere it as such. We acknowledge our debt to Russell L. Ackoff, C. West Churchman, Thomas A. Cowan, and Robert Tannenbaum. We are also indebted to our colleagues and friends Chris Argyris, Paul Diesing, Gerald Gordon, Richard O. Mason, Louis Pondy, Vern Taylor, Kenneth W. Thomas, William Torbert, and Gerald Zaltman. Finally, we wish to acknowledge our greatest colleagues of all, our wives, Donna Mitroff and Audrey Kilmann, with whom we have discussed many of the concepts in this book and to whose critical insights we are indebted. Both have a deep interest in social science and in the development of a unified human science.

Pittsburgh, Pennsylvania IAN I. MITROFF
August 1978 RALPH H. KILMANN

Contents

The Authors

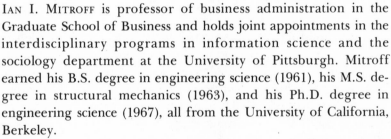

IAN I. MITROFF is professor of business administration in the Graduate School of Business and holds joint appointments in the interdisciplinary programs in information science and the sociology department at the University of Pittsburgh. Mitroff earned his B.S. degree in engineering science (1961), his M.S. degree in structural mechanics (1963), and his Ph.D. degree in engineering science (1967), all from the University of California, Berkeley.

Ian Mitroff's current research interests include strategic planning models, theories of real-world problem solving, science policy studies, general systems theory and design, and management information systems. At the University of Pittsburgh, Mitroff has served as a research associate in the Philosophy of Science Center and as program director and research associate at the Learning Research and Development Center. During 1977, Mitroff was visiting professor of business administration and social systems science at the Wharton School of the University of Pennsylvania. The American Psychological Association, the Philosophy of Science Association, and the Institute for Management Science are among the professional associations in which he is active.

Mitroff is the author of *The Subjective Side of Science: A Philosophical Inquiry into the Psychology of the Apollo Moon Scientists* (1974). He has also published numerous articles concerning such areas as the social psychology of science and technology and the methodology and philosophy of social science in *Management Science, Human Relations, Philosophy of Social Science,* and other journals.

Mitroff and his wife. Donna, live in Pittsburgh with their daughter, Dana. Their hobbies include running, cross-country skiing, and visiting their farm in West Virginia.

RALPH H. KILMANN is associate professor of business administration in the Graduate School of Business at the University of Pittsburgh. He earned both his B.S. degree in administrative and management science and his M.S. degree in industrial administration at Carnegie-Mellon University (1970). He received his Ph.D. degree in management from the University of California, Los Angeles (1972).

Ralph Kilmann's research interests include the design of organizations and institutions, organizational problem solving, conflict management, strategic planning and policy analysis, and how these behavioral concepts can be applied to study the conduct and institution of science. He is an active member of several professional organizations, including the American Psychological Association and the Academy of Management. Kilmann was corecipient for first prize in the Institute of Management Science's 1976 competition for the best case study in planning. Since 1975, he has been president of Organizational Design Consultants, a Pittsburgh-based firm specializing in the development and application of the Multivariate Analysis, Participation, and Structure (MAPS) Design Technology.

Kilmann is the author of *Social Systems Design: Normative Theory and The MAPS Design Technology* (1977) and an editor of *The Management of Organization Design: Volumes I and II* (with L. R. Pondy and D. P. Slevin, 1976). He codeveloped the *Thomas-Kilmann Conflict-Mode Instrument* (1974) and has published over fifty articles in such journals as *Administrative Science Quarterly, Journal of Applied Psychology, Human Relations, Academy of Management Journal* and *Management Science.*

Kilmann is married to Audrey Ann and has a daughter, Catherine Mary. His hobbies include running, automobiles, photography, and classical music.

To our parents

Methodological Approaches to Social Science

*Integrating Divergent
Concepts and Theories*

ONE

The Crisis of
Scientific Belief

*There is no sound reason why [an] inquiring system should "start"
with logic. To be sure, all inquiry uses logic, but then, . . . all
inquiry uses every branch of inquiry. Logic itself can be regarded
as a derivation of social communication, that is, as a branch of
sociology.*

> *All of the recent hue and cry for "interdisciplinary
research" by foundations and other supporters of science might be
regarded as a response to the collective unconscious realization
that human knowledge does not come in pieces: To understand an
aspect of nature is to see it through "all" the ways of imagery.*

C. West Churchman (1971, p. 198)

In recent years, the institution of science has come under increasing, if not severe, attack. In many senses, this attack is neither new nor unexpected. Since its very inception, as one of mankind's most important and cherished institutions, science has been severely criticized. Two aspects of the current denunciations differentiate them from earlier ones and make them deserving of serious attention. The first has to do with the intensity of the attacks, the second with the scope of the attacks.

Science has always depended on many external institutions for its support, and occasionally its relations become strained with the very institutions on which it depends. For example, the U.S. Congress has questioned the fairness of the internal peer review procedures that the National Science Foundation (NSF) uses to select research projects deemed worthy of support. Since the NSF is supported by public monies, Congress has every right to inquire into whether these funds are being equitably distributed to applicants irrespective of such factors as the prestige of individual applicants or their affiliations, age, or sex. Of special concern to the Congress is whether the NSF peer review acts to suppress— consciously or unconsciously—novel ideas that challenge the mainstream of scientific thought. (In a study by Hensler (1976), over 50 percent of reviewers and past applicants for NSF grants who were sampled believed that, given two proposals which were identical in every respect save that one challenged the mainstream of current thought and the other did not, the nonchallenging proposal stood a much better chance of being funded.)

Although the foregoing concerns may account for some of the criticism directed toward the NSF, they are far from sufficient to account for its intensity, which suggests to us a significant turn in the relationship of science to the larger society. We cannot prove beyond all doubt that the criticism represents a new relationship, but we do believe that it is symptomatic of a slowly emerging trend—a growing disillusionment and disenchantment with the nature of scientific enterprise. A careful reading of the U.S. Congress proceedings on the NSF peer review processes clearly reveals that representatives are not only asking hard and critical questions about the NSF's methods but also about whether science is really all that it has traditionally been cracked up to be. For example, "Is there an old-boy network that acts to favor some scientists? Do the rich get richer? Do innovative ideas fare well?" (See U.S. Congress, 1976; and Mitroff and Chubin, n.d.) The recent general decline in trust and confidence in a large number of society's institutions has spread to science.

This lack of confidence would be easier to bear were it confined solely to those persons and institutions external to science. However, a number of eminent scientists and social thinkers have expressed grave doubts regarding the very nature of science itself—at least the kind of science we have known. Serious arguments have been advanced that there are major defects inherent in the structure of science itself and in our conception of it as a method of inquiry. Some thinkers have contended that science is in serious need of reform in its characteristic ways of knowing—its methodology—and in what it pretends to know about the world— its epistemology. Still others have argued for nearly complete or total renunciation of science as the standard for material progress and knowing, and the substitution of other, possibly older and more fundamental, ways of knowing (Roszak, 1973).

Although we feel that some of the criticisms regarding science are misguided and wrong, we do think the crisis is real. The critics are pointing to some serious defects, which are rooted deeply in the structure of science. Our view is that science is in serious need of methodological and epistemological reform. Even if there were no "crisis of belief" in science, there would still be good reasons for considering reform at this time, given the new cultural forces and streams of thought being articulated. We are, in short, on the edge of a revolution with regard to our thinking about the character of science, and the time is ripe for serious thought about the directions in which this revolution should proceed. Further, the nature of this revolution is intimately tied to the fate of the social or "human" sciences. The main reason why the social sciences have given a fragmentary and incomplete account of the nature of man is that the social sciences have themselves been conceived of and practiced largely in a fragmentary and incomplete manner. An account of the social sciences that recognizes and attempts to capitalize on the intense differences in style between the practitioners of different schools of social science is thus called for.

Fundamentally, this book attempts to turn the social psychology of science on its head. Sufficient knowledge can be derived from the psychology and the sociology of science to identify distinct basic patterns of inquiry practiced by different kinds of scientists. Some of these patterns are old and clearly recognizable; others are new and still struggling for emergence and recognition.

We are not the first to raise these issues. In a recent book, *Where the Wasteland Ends* (1973), Theodore Roszak argues that understanding and coming to grips with the psychology underlying modern science is currently the most critical problem facing Western civilization. Roszak's argument runs as follows: Western civilization has become increasingly dependent upon modern science not only in order to satisfy its material needs (some of which were created by science itself) but also for its basic philosophy of knowing. Science has become not only the standard for doing (material progress) but for knowing as well (epistemological progress). We should then take a very serious look at the psychology underlying science. What are the psychological forces and impulses undergirding modern science? What attributes of mind have let science become what it is? Further, if there are defects in our ways of knowing and doing, are they traceable back to the qualities of mind underlying it? Is science largely the creation and dominance of a particular psychological type of style, the projection of a particular psyche, onto the world? And if so, are alternate forms of science based on alternate psychological styles possible? We believe the answer to the preceding questions is "yes."

The rest of this chapter explicates some of the features or dimensions that characterize both established and newly emerging patterns of inquiry. The features we will discuss are necessary but neither individually nor collectively sufficient to characterize fully a pattern of inquiry. Indeed, the question of sufficiency must remain open at this time; we must confine ourselves to those features we see as important and within our sphere of competency. Sufficiency conditions cannot be derived from any single science or scientist because they cut across all of the sciences currently known and depend upon our ability to develop more complete transdisciplinary sciences and scientists. The construction of an adequate set of sufficiency conditions is a systemic effort, not a disciplinary one.

In a sense, our enterprise revolves around the construction of a typology capable of identifying basic styles of thinking about and doing science. In Chapter Two, we engage in a critical, selective review of the literature in the psychology and sociology of science in order to develop such a typology. The construction of an adequate typology, with the clear identificiation of its underlying dimensions, constitutes the first and necessary component of our overall objective. Everything that follows is dependent upon this critical first task; hence, the special attention we pay to it in the next chapter.

In particular, five features derive from our review of the various literatures in the philosophy, psychology, and sociology of science. We view these features as necessary to any style of inquiry. First, each style has a preferred set of *logic,* or in some cases a single logic, which it accepts either implicitly or unconsciously. Conversely, each style often rejects other sets of logic, again either consciously or unconsciously.

Today there exist a number of modern alternatives to classical Aristotelian logic, which emphasized the strict truth or falsity of particular propositions. Some of these alternative logics or patterns of reasoning are more naturally associated with some styles of inquiry than with others. Some logics insist upon a determination of the truth or falsity of a proposition. Others maintain that certain propositions are neither true nor false in the strict conventional sense but "indeterminate," that is neither true nor false. The most radical are the dialectical logics, which contend that a proposition and its negation can both be true or false at the same time.

We shall pay special attention to these dialectical logics for three reasons: (1) Two of the styles of inquiry we shall examine in depth are dialectical in their reasoning processes. Thus dialectical logic is both appropriate and necessary for capturing the style of reasoning characteristic of these two styles. (2) There is a natural dialectic operating not only within some of the styles (a microdialectic) but also between the styles (a macrodialectic). (3) One of the reasons the social sciences have failed to do justice to the complex phenomenon called "humanity" is that they have failed to capture the complex patterns of reasoning of which humans are capable. In other words, a social theory must be explicitly dialectical in its constitution if it is ever to do justice to the central phenomenon of its interest—mankind. Furthermore, this dialectic must not be merely abstract or conceptual; it must become an integral part of the methodology of social science that studies human thought.

A second feature necessary to a style of inquiry is that each style must be capable of accounting for *rational, nonrational,* and *irrational characteristics.* "Irrational" is usually thought of as "opposed to rational"; it isolates conventions of rational. To be "nonrational" is to be either unconcerned with rationality or beyond its pale; one is on another plane as it were. Each style of inquiry is made up of a combination of these aspects. No matter what standard of rationality we use, every style of inquiry has both rational and irrational features. By focusing on either the rational or the irrational to the exclusion of the other, we present and perpetuate a distorted image of each style. Paul Diesing's *Reason in Society* (1962) is one of the best expositions of this thesis. Diesing summarizes and contrasts in depth four different types of rationality: (1) social, (2) legal, (3) political, and (4) economic. While very different from (sometimes hostile to) one another, each of the four would soon wither away without the others. Each form of rationality is vitally dependent on the others but takes them entirely for granted.

Modern psychological and sociological research has clearly revealed the existence of both rational and irrational, objective and subjective factors operating within the institution of science and within individual scientists (Mitroff, 1974a, 1974b). To require a theory of science to account for both aspects does not make one a subjectivist or an irrationalist or, for that matter, an objectivist or a rationalist. It simply attempts to give a fuller and more complete picture of the workings of individual scientists and of science as an institution.

A third feature necessary to a style of inquiry is that it must attempt to represent as many of the *component processes of the inquiry* as possible. For example, each style must describe its procedures for both the discovery of a scientific hypothesis, model, or theory and its subsequent testing. That is, discovery and testing are both components of any style of inquiry. This feature is related to the preceding one; for, as we shall see, some styles of inquiry see discovery as irrational and testing as rational and the two as clearly separable from one another. Others see both as either rational or irrational and nonseparable or even indistinguishable.

The fourth feature of styles of inquiry concerns the *institutional or social norms* of science they embody. Each style of inquiry has a different set of preferred social norms under which it operates. Some styles embody the traditional norms of science portrayed by such thinkers as Merton (1968) and Barber (1952). Others embody nontraditional norms (Merton, 1968, 1969; Mitroff, 1974a, 1974b). Still other styles focus on norms not identified at all by previous discussions.

The fifth and most important feature of a style of inquiry is its set of *concrete methodological rules* specific to the preferred kinds of inquiries associated with the style. Our attempt to define specific methodologies for the design, conduct, and evaluation of social science inquiry should lead to a set of explicit alternatives for the conduct of inquiry. Without such explicit alternatives, the newly emerging forms of inquiry will not receive the attention they deserve, nor will scientists be able to choose intelligently the style of inquiry best suited to their purposes.

It has become fashionable of late to talk of *contingency models* in the social sciences (Gordon and others, 1974). Our attempt is to fashion a contingency model of scientific methodology, that is, to spell out the different rules and criteria governing each inquiry style so that the scientist can answer the vital question: "Which inquiry style should I adopt in order to best serve my overall experimental purposes?" Unless the rules governing each style are identified, the practicing scientist may have no choice but to adopt those styles whose rules have been codified to the greatest degree. This would be unfortunate, for the degree of codification of a style of inquiry should not be the sole criterion guiding its selection.

The foregoing discussion hardly exhausts all of the features associated with a style of inquiry. One could include the "rhetoric of everyday presentation" of a style of inquiry or its linguistic structure. These features and others will be touched upon in the following chapters, for each style is distinguished by its semantics, syntax, empirics, and pragmatics.

It should be apparent by now that this book itself attempts to practice a different style of inquiry—to show what the various social sciences have to contribute to one another. In fact, we attempt to show that the separate sciences depend upon each other in countless ways and can no longer afford to proceed in isolation from one another.

This is the place to answer the charges of subjectivism, psychologicism, and sociologicism so often hurled at any effort that attempts to integrate the logical with the psychological and the sociological. We do not claim that psychology and sociology are more fundamental than logic and somehow determine or prescribe logic. Rather, we contend that logic, psychology, and sociology can no longer afford to proceed in their respective vacuums. This issue is illustrated by the following quotes from writers who clearly anticipated our themes and to whom, as a result, we are in debt.

Harré and Secord, in their thought-provoking book *The Explanation of Social Behavior* (1973, p. 2), write: "In our view, an adequate social psychology can be developed only as a cooperative enterprise between psychologists, philosophers, and sociologists. No one of these groups seems able to be successful alone. Psychologists have often been concerned with too narrow a conception of social action, and have been severely handicapped by conceptual naivete. Philosophers have not lacked conceptual sophistication but have too often been ignorant of social and psychological facts, while sociologists, despite great breadth of conception, have been unable to develop adequate theories of individual social action, and have suffered, with psychologists, from conceptual naivete. We hope that in this study some of these difficulties can be ameliorated by collaboration."

John Dewey, in *Explanation of Social Behavior* (1953, pp. 326–327), responds to charges of subjectivism as follows:

> Because Mr. William James recognizes that the personal element enters into judgments . . . he is charged with extreme subjectivism, with encouraging the element of personal preference to run roughshod over all objective controls. . . . The question raised . . . is primarily one of fact, not of doctrine. Is or is not a personal factor found in truth evaluations? . . . The moment complicity of the personal factor is recognized fully, frankly, and generally, that moment a new era in philosophy will begin. We shall have to discover the personal factors that now influence us unconsciously, and begin to accept a new and moral responsibility for them, a responsibility for judging and testing them by their consequences. So long as we ignore this factor, its deeds will be largely evil, not because *it* is evil, but because, flourishing in the dark, it is without responsibility and without check. The only way to control it is by recognizing it.

As Dewey, and more contemporary thinkers such as Churchman (1971), continually remind us, logic, psychology, and sociology are not three separate sciences but three aspects—three different ways of studying—the same thing: the nature of knowledge and its relationship to a knowing entity. Depending upon our objective they may even be regarded as subsets of one another. Thus, logic can be regarded as a form of social communication; psychology and sociology as particular ways of ordering thought. The purpose of this book is to take these long-overdue suggestions seriously and to develop them in more detail.

A transdisciplinary view of scientific styles of inquiry—a view not only of differences and similarities between styles but of the consequences of the styles themselves—is not merely an interesting topic of discussion. Indeed, such a view is vital if we are to avoid a breakdown in the vigor of the social sciences as fields of endeavor. The possible consequences of the currently increasing disparity among the social sciences are numerous and dire: breakdown of communications between different fields of inquiry, overlap and waste of diminishing time and resources, a trend away from humanism in the sciences, even eventual social chaos. Resolution of the disparity among the social sciences, although no guarantee of a smooth social improvement, at least offers the possibility of more efficient and effective use of human resources in solving problems of the quality of human life.

TWO

How Scientists Classify Scientists

*Ultimately, I am convinced we shall have to include in the
education of the young scientist both the techniques of caution and
of boldness. Mere caution and soberness, mere compulsiveness can
produce only good technicians who are much less likely to discover
or invent new truths or new theories. The caution, patience, and
conservatism which are sine qua non for the scientist had better
be supplemented by boldness and daring if creativeness is also the
hope. Both are necessary. They need not be mutually exclusive. They
can be integrated with each other. Taken together they constitute
flexibility, adaptability, versatility.*

Abraham Maslow (1966, pp. 31–32)

In this chapter we will construct a typology of the major ways in
which social scientists think about and practice science. First we
review a select sample of five typologies that have actually been
proposed by particular scientists for describing scientific styles of
inquiry. This review can be described as a "typology of scientific
typologies." We then go on to extract a set of basic dimensions
common to the five typologies to serve as the basis of our own
typology, which is then analyzed in depth in Chapters Three through
Six. The importance of an adequate typology of scientific inquiry
cannot be overemphasized. Indeed, we believe that a clear view of

the different ways of thinking about science is essential to our over-all goal of proposing a unified methodology for the social sciences. To date, not enough attention has been given to the styles of in-quiry that fundamentally different kinds of scientists manifest in their day-to-day practice of science. Although the more traditional studies regarding the educational, family, and religious backgrounds and origins of scientists are by no means unimportant (see Eiduson and Beckman, 1973), the relatively little attention paid to studying the differences in inquiry, cognitive, and epis-temological styles between scientists is indeed disturbing. As a result, in this study we are interested in the general demographic and background characteristics of scientists only insofar as they illuminate or explain differences in style.

Three preliminary assumptions underlie the "typology of typologies" that follows. First, we do not see the construction of a typology as an exercise in compulsive categorizing, nor do we wish to assign each and every scientist to one and only one style. This is consistent neither with good typology nor with human nature. A good typology should not reduce people down to single "types." Rather, it should serve as a signpost to help us to see and to or-ganize some of the complex patterns by which humans behave. (See Diesing, 1971, for a detailed discussion of the benefits and the difficulties of typology construction.) Indeed, we emphasize that real people do not fit into any one type precisely because of their diverse, sometimes contrary attributes. Any personality is marked as much by its inconsistencies as by its consistencies. (See Jung, 1968; 1971 for further explanation.)

Our second assumption is that the attributes of any particu-lar type are not to be seen as immutable traits. Each type should instead by viewed as a broad style or cluster of potential attributes that can and often will vary depending on the particular situation.

The third assumption is that every typology is by nature limited in the number of types it allows for. Although our own typology has four major styles of scientific inquiry, we do not imply that four and only four types are sufficient to describe the variety of styles exhibited by the complex body of social scientists. As one of our mentors, T.A. Cowan, so often put it, "There are two kinds of people in the world; those who believe there are two kinds of people and those who don't." We hope we are of the second "type"—those who do *not* believe that there are two and only two (or four and only four) kinds of people in the world. For now, we merely wish to emphasize that we shall deal with only four distinct types for reasons of convenience. Also for reasons of convenience, we will deliberately exaggerate the features of each type for better contrast. As we shall point out, the greatest scientists seem not only to combine the attributes of opposing types but to delight in doing so. In Jung's and Maslow's terms, the healthiest personalities are characterized by their transcendence of any one personality system.

Our fourth assumption is that no one type is eminently more desirable than the others. It is very tempting in constructing a typology to see one or more of the types in a more favorable light. For example, this work tends to be very critical of the Analytic Scientist described in Chapter Three, in part as a reflection of our own personal preferences, and also because this work is in the style of the Conceptual Theorist described in Chapter Four. It should be realized that every style of inquiry has both strong and weak points. Every style becomes detrimental when pushed to extreme limits. However one should not mistake the distorted extreme form of a type for the whole of that type and reject it altogether. We will take special pains not to let this happen to us in our descriptions.

We turn now to a sample of five specific typologies in the sociology and psychology of science, each of which pays particular attention not only to the characteristics of each type but also to the general dimensions each system introduces to differentiate between different types of scientists. These typologies have been selected for detailed discussion because of their clarity in presenting different styles of doing science. (Two of the typologies—those of Liam Hudson and Abraham Maslow—go beyond mere description to speculate on the psychodynamic origins of the styles of inquiry.) The five typologies are presented in order of their relative complexity, beginning with Liam Hudson's relatively simple two-part typology and progressing through the more detailed, multi-faceted typologies. No qualitative progression is intended by this ordering. The personality typology of C. G. Jung is presented fifth because it serves as the foundation of our own typology, which is discussed in the final section of this chapter.

The Typology of Liam Hudson

By almost any standard, Liam Hudson's *Contrary Imaginations* (1966) is a remarkable book. Deceptively short and eminently readable, it offers a wealth of factual detail, interesting theoretical arguments, and fascinating speculations about two kinds of British schoolboys, convergers and divergers. The converger tends to go into the sciences, principally the physical and natural sciences; the diverger tends to go into the humanities, politics, law, and the social sciences (that is, when psychology is conceived of as a social or human science and not strictly as a branch of natural science). As we shall see, those two types of schoolboys are noticeably different not only in their sensitivity to detail, facts, and preferences for global or holistic thinking but also in their emotional lives and their styles of creativity.

One of the strong points of Hudson's typology is that it stresses the mutual usefulness (indeed the interdependency) of converger and diverger. It is definitely not the case that one type is better or more creative than the other. Rather, each compensates for the blind or the weak points of the other; each embodies a different aspect of creativity.

The major characteristics of convergers are their extreme sensitivity to and preference for gathering impersonal facts and details with regard to any situation. They are analysts *par excellence*. They are more realistic and reductionistic in their thinking than they are idealistic or holistic. Their approach to any situation is to break it down into component parts and to treat each component as an independent, isolated fact. Convergers tend to repeat this process of breaking each part down into other parts, sometimes to extremes.

Convergers tend to do well on standardized tests, which require the subject (or the "victim," as Hudson prefers) to choose or *converge* on the single right answer to a question. Convergers do well on tasks that are well structured and have a clearly defined formulation and answer. In fact, convergers sometimes even structure problems so as to appear or become well structured. Convergers have a low tolerance for ambiguity; in the extreme, they despise ambiguous situations.

The major characteristics of divergers are their extreme sensitivity to and preference for inventing personal global descriptions in response to any situation. Divergers are expansive storytellers *par excellence.* They are much more idealistic and holistic in their thinking than realistic or reductionistic. Their approach to any situation is to create an ever-expanding global portrait. The tendency of divergers is to expand, encompass, and create ever-expanding totalities of experiences, sensations, dreams, stories— sometimes to extremes.

Divergers do not tend to do well on standardized tests, but they do well on tasks that do not call for a single, unambiguous, "correct" answer but instead require them to invent a number of new possibilities. They are not only tolerant of ambiguity but relish the creation of ambiguity or diversity, even when it appears contradictory.

The emotional lives of these two types are also very different. Divergers display their emotions much more readily than do convergers. This does not mean that convergers have no feelings, but they have much more control of their emotions than do divergers. One of the main tasks that Hudson (1966) used to differentiate between convergers and divergers was the number of different uses they could think of for common, everyday objects such as a barrel, a paper clip, a brick, a blanket, and so forth. Not only did convergers produce significantly fewer uses for each object than divergers, but out of the twenty-five most frequently selected morbid or bizarre uses, the first eight items were produced by convergers. Further, "the most 'morbid' responses from divergers all seem relatively innocuous when one compares them with the first half-dozen or so on the list (for example, using a brick to smash one's sister's head in, or using a barrel to stuff headless bodies in, versus using a blanket to suffocate a person)" (Hudson, 1966, p. 60).

Because of the importance of Hudson's findings and interpretations, it is helpful to quote him directly: "If we accept [the] idea of a mental barrier, a great deal about the converger makes sense. We note, for example, that his reactions to controversial issues are often stereotyped, and that he is prone to compartmentalize one topic from another. Both habits of mind serve, presumably, to minimize the uneasiness which ambiguous or conflicting ideas create; and both may be seen as defenses against anxiety.

Both stereotyping and compartmentalizing serve to keep unpleasant conflicts at bay, and do so by the primitive expedient of ignoring them . . . . Many convergers, one suspects, do not stifle strong, disorganized, feelings—they fail to experience them" (1966, p. 85). The diverger has his weaknesses too: "The chief of these lies in his reaction to precise, logical argument. He is weak at this, and in some cases, seems positively alarmed by it. Where the converger enjoys precision (and the lack of ambiguity), the diverger views it as a trap. In caricature, the converger takes refuge from people in things; the diverger takes refuge from things in people" (1966, p. 91).

As to the underlying causes for convergers and divergers having become what they are, one can only speculate (a divergent attribute) because we do not possess sufficient data to decide unequivocally (a convergent characteristic).

The danger of the converger's approach is that it threatens to deny the very existence of emotions precisely because emotions cannot be precisely defined or quantitatively measured. The danger of the diverger's position is that it threatens to imbue everything with emotion, thus denying the reality of external, objective reality.

The creativity of the diverger is not to be seen as superior to that of the converger. Within certain traditions in Western culture divergence and creativity have become virtually synonymous with one another, and the converger is not granted any creativity at all. Hudson is to be applauded for resisting this easy temptation. Both convergers and divergers can be either creative or uncreative. Convergers, when they are creative, are creative within a single ordered framework. Their creativity consists in developing an idea precisely and deeply within a deep, elaborate structure. Divergers, when they are creative, are creative across diverse patterns of thought rather than ordered frameworks. The creativity of the diverger is akin to that of the artist or the broad conceptual thinker, whose creativity consists of seeing whole new visions—of visualizing whole new ways of looking at things—but not necessarily of working them out in detail.

It is important to emphasize that Hudson's terms *diverger* and *converger* represent the end points of a spectrum: "Working from one end of the distribution to the other, we find extreme divergers (10 percent); moderate divergers (20 percent); all-rounders (40 percent); moderate convergers (20 percent); and extreme convergers (10 percent)" (1966, p. 41). We believe, however, that it might be more useful to realize that divergence and convergence are complex dimensions rather than simply a single continuum. An individual may be high in either dimension or high in both or low in both. Hudson's "all-rounders" may be low in both divergence and convergence and therefore unlikely to go into any aspect of the sciences. The rarest type is that individual who is high in both; such a person, as we shall see, may be the ultimate integrator of scientific approaches.

It may appear strange that we have paid so much attention to a typology of British schoolboys rather than mature working scientists. It may also appear that the typology is better suited for treating the differences between scientists and artists than between kinds of scientists. Both of these impressions, however, are wrong. The differences we have been examining hold for mature working scientists and between different kinds of scientists. We can identify the converger with the Apollonian scientist and the diverger with the Dionysian scientist, as so aptly described by the Nobelist Szent-Gyorgyi in his important letter to *Science* magazine (1972). Finally, there is a marked advantage of a typology that deals explicitly with schoolboys instead of mature working scientists. Since schoolboys, even of ages fifteen to seventeen, are closer to childhood and hence to parental influences than mature scientists, we are free to question early causative influences on their styles of inquiry, even if the ultimate answer to the question of causation must remain speculative at this time (Hudson, 1966).

The Typology of Gerald Gordon

The work of Gerald Gordon and his colleagues and students is important for a number of reasons. First, it pertains to the cognitive styles of working scientists. Second, it contains a greater number of types than does Hudson's typology of convergers and divergers. While more types are not desirable per se, it does allow one to make more refined distinctions between different types of scientists. Third, the dimensions of Gordon's typology are based on a clearer identification of underlying dimensions, whereas the dimensions underlying Hudson's typology are multidimensional. Thus, with Gordon's typology it is easier to identify precisely the specific attributes or dimensions on which particular scientists differ from one another. Fourth, and most important, Gordon has not been content merely to measure the cognitive styles of working scientists; he has gone on to link the cognitive style of scientists with their scientific performance, affording some external validation of the concept of a cognitive style—whether it stands up to theoretical predictions.

Gordon and his colleagues set out to study the factors conducive to innovative scientific problem solving within organizations. As might be expected, both individual psychological factors and social or organizational factors played an important role. If an organization lacked the proper structure, even a highly innovative individual would be blocked by the organization's structure or working climate. Conversely, if an organization contained the proper structure, innovativeness would be lacking in the absence of innovative individuals.

Gordon and his colleagues see two abilities as important to an individual's propensity to innovate: the ability to differentiate among stimuli and the ability to make remote associations—to form meaningful patterns between diverse and seemingly unrelated stimuli. Those who have the ability to differentiate among stimuli are called high social differentiators (High Diff.). As Gordon and Morse put it:

> High differentiators perceive their environment as a series of discrete parts while low differentiators see their environment as highly homogeneous. The high differentiators welcome differences in the environment while low differentiators overlook or reject them. The ability to differentiate manifests itself in two related ways depending on the nature of the stimulus, human or inanimate. In interacting with people, the high differentiator perceives and reacts to each as a unique individual possessing a combination of capabilities and inabilities. The low differentiator perceives people as being more or less alike and thus tends to suppress or ignore individual capabilities. Behavior patterns of the high and low differentiators also differ on their responses to inanimate objects such as information concerning their environment. . . . The low differentiator seems to be so rigidly bound by his preconceived notions that he ignores or suppresses stimuli which are not consistent with his preconceptions. The high differentiator, on the

other hand, is sensitive to inconsistencies and appears to welcome diversity. To the extent to which creating (a new theory) requires a person able to respond effectively to diverse bits of information and subtle cues about the environment and to identify problems, the need for social differentiation is apparent [1969, p. 43].

However, perception alone, differentiated or not, is not always sufficient for innovative problem solving: "If normal solutions do not suffice, it becomes necessary, as Mednick has pointed out, for someone to perceive meaningful and useful relations in seemingly disparate data and come up with a unique solution. Employing this theory Mednick constructed the Remote Associates Test (RAT) to measure creative potential. In the test a person is given a series of three words such as cheese, blood, and water and is asked to think up a fourth word which is common to all three words. In this case the word is blue" (1969, p. 45).

Gordon and Morse's contention, which is borne out by their studies, is that the RAT. measures a person's ability to solve a predetermined problem but not the ability to recognize unformed problems. This is the function of high differentiation. The contention is that both abilities play an important role in innovative problem solving. On the basis of these ideas, Gordon and Morse identified four theoretical kinds of scientists or styles of scientific problem solving:

- Type 1—Integrators (High Diff. and High RAT)
- Type 2—Problem Solvers (Low Diff. and High RAT)
- Type 3—Problem Recognizers (High Diff. and Low RAT)
- Type 4—Technicians (Low Diff. and Low RAT)

Integrators supposedly possess both the ability to recognize previously unperceived problems (high differentiation) and the technical skills to solve problems once they are recognized (High RAT). Problem Solvers (High RAT), in contrast, possess the ability to solve already formulated problems but lack the ability to recognize new problems (low differentation). Problem Recognizers are just the reverse of Problem Solvers. Technicians possess neither the ability to recognize new problems nor to solve any but the most standardized problem. Thus Gordon and Morse postulated that Integrators would be the most innovative, Technicians the least; in addition Integrators would require the least supervision, Technicians the most.

With very minor exceptions, these predictions were borne out with studies of industrial scientists. Integrators were the most successful in applying for and securing patents; Problem Solvers were next, and so on. Even more powerful was the finding that in research groups led by Integrators, the performance of all the types improved, whereas in groups led by Problem Solvers, the performance of all the types suffered: "The high differentiator [should be the] administrative superior and . . . information [should] be channeled through him. . . . The high differentiator's ability to recognize and react to persons around him as unique individuals with abilities and inabilities enables him to effectively delegate tasks and resources on the basis of an individual's differential capacity to deal with various kinds of problems. Further, the high differentiator is sensitive to inconsistencies and has a propensity to stress differences in data, thus increasing the availability of different types of data needed to make remote associations. Giving the High RAT–low differentiator [the Problem Solver] control over information would probably result in the rejection of inconsistencies in data, thus inhibiting the innovative process" 1969, pp. 48–49).

Gordon and Morse's Technician corresponds to Hudson's extreme converger (high convergence, low divergence); in fact, the Technician represents the most extreme converger of all—so extreme or narrow that he must be guided in what to do. Convergence becomes dysfunctional at this point because whatever positive attributes convergence possesses, become muted and lost. Gordon and Morse's Problem Solvers correspond to Hudson's moderate convergers (moderate convergence, low divergence). The Integrator corresponds to Hudson's "all-rounders," with the very important exception that Gordon and Morse's Integrator seems to combine aspects of both extreme divergence and extreme convergence simultaneously. The Problem Recognizer corresponds to the moderate or extreme diverger (low convergence, moderate to high divergence).

More important than one-to-one correspondence between typologies is the fact that in other work, Gordon and others (1974) have made use of his types to construct a most interesting contingency model of science specifying which types seem best suited for working on various aspects of the scientific problem solving or inquiry process. We will discuss this contingency model in detail in Chapter Seven.

Mitroff's Survey of the Apollo Scientists

Mitroff (1974a, 1974b, 1977) has described the results of a four-year extensive study of forty-two of the most prestigious scientists who studied the Apollo moon rocks. Mitroff's study revealed intense differences between the way scientists approach their work. Even more important, it revealed that scientists themselves are aware of such differences, often think about them, and some have even constructed operationally significant typologies of their own. Although we feel that all of the types have an extremely important function to play in science, scientists in general do not always feel this way. A number of the scientists Mitroff interviewed emphasized that they would be happy to see certain scientists (different from themselves) disappear altogether because of what those interviewed deemed offensive behavioral characteristics. This ultimate act of disapprobation—for one scientist to say he no longer regards another scientist as a scientist—represents the mutual intolerance and hostility between different types of scientists that have motivated the writing of this book.* We feel that the divergence between different approaches to science in Western culture has reached the point at which a serious attempt at reconciliation is vital.

The study of the moon scientists was conducted in four interview rounds. The interviews were carefully designed to explore technical issues, such as how the views of the scientists regarding the moon's origin and detailed properties changed over time as

*The traditional use of the pronoun *he* has not yet been superseded by a convenient, generally accepted pronoun meaning *he* or *she*. The authors will continue to use he but wish to acknowledge the inherent inequity of the traditional preference of the masculine pronoun.

data came in from the Apollo missions, and especially sensitive issues, such as what the scientists thought about one another as scientists and as people. For example, each of the forty-two scientists was specifically asked which scientists they thought would have the most difficulty in changing their personal beliefs regarding the origin of the moon and other scientific issues. Three particular scientists were believed by virtually the entire sample to be most committed to their ideas and therefore expected to have the most difficulty in parting with them.

During the course of discussion on scientists' commitment to their ideas, two scientists volunteered their own typologies of scientists. For convenience, we shall merely report on one of these typologies which consists of three types. We do not claim any special validity for the typology just because it was volunteered; we do claim that it is important to observe what practicing scientists themselves believe. When those surveyed were asked to rank the forty-two scientists according to this typology, a highly consistent pattern of nominations was made for representatives for each of the types. In later interviews when the scientists were asked to give quantitative ratings of the scientists on various scales, a highly consistent pattern again emerged which tended to give needed support to the validity of the typology. The scientists also agreed with the basic dimensions and the types of the typology.

There are three types to the typology, unpoetically referred to as Types I, II, and III. (Note that this is typical of a converger's approach, the depersonalization of human attributes by reducing them to numbers.) The basic dimension underlying the typology is speculativeness. Type I scientists are distinguished by their extreme willingness to speculate far afield from known data, or even ignore data when the situation demanded it, in order to construct highly imaginative conceptual theories. Type I scientists are not formal mathematical theorists but conceptual theorists of the first rank. They enjoy finding and creating patterns in disparate data drawn from the most widely scattered scientific fields. Type III scientists represent the other end of the continuum. Here, speculation is disdained and avoided at almost any cost. Type III scientists value precision and fine experimental work above all else. Type

III's believe in "sticking close to the data." Theories may come and go but good scientific data will last forever. (Gordon and Morse would call Type III's Problem Solvers or even Technicians.)

The Type II represents something in between—capable both of doing good experimental work and of speculating modestly on it, or better yet, interpreting it. At times, Type II scientists might even rise to bold speculation; however, they are more akin to Problem Solvers than to Problem Recognizers or Integrators.

The vast majority of scientists in the sample were Type II's, so it is not surprising that Type II's were most popular among them. This does not mean that I's and III's were unrepresented completely, but they were rare, especially Type I's, the conceptual theorists. Only three scientists were consistently designated Type I, and these same three scientists were the most prestigious in terms of recognition, awards, and position. Surprisingly, these scientists were also viewed as the most obstinate: they are the very same three scientists who were earlier viewed as the most committed to their hypotheses!

The Type III scientists in the sample were viewed as "number crunchers," "unimaginative clods," "the average scientist," and worse. The point is that the most outstanding scientists—those who best typify Kuhn's revoluntionary scientist (1962)—belie the stereotypical portrait of the scientist (Mitroff, 1974b). They are not unbiased, objective, neutral observers of nature; rather, they are highly partisan advocates of the theories they are developing. Indeed, the Type III scientist—who is viewed as uncreative, unimaginative, dull—is for this very reason judged unbiased. He is a narrow specialist who comes closest to the stereotypical portrait of the scientist. In fact, it was the consensus of the sample that in order to be a good scientist one had to be committed to one's theories. Nearly the entire sample scoffed at the notion of the unbiased, objective scientist. According to these scientists, the only people who take that notion seriously are the "unknowing" public and first-year science students. Real, practicing scientists know better. They do science every day; they live in close contact with Type I's and see how they operate. A very different picture of science emerges from this survey. Given the long history of myths surrounding science, it may be overdue. Later we shall have more to say about this and what it implies for the traditional concepts of scientific objectivity.

The Typology of Abraham Maslow

In the strict sense, Maslow does not present a formal typology of scientists as have the previous writers discussed. However, there is an underlying typology operating in his powerful book, *The Psychology of Science* (1966), in which Maslow continually contrasts and compares two kinds of scientists and by implication two very different kinds of science: healthy and creative science, which promotes the growth of the individual scientist as a human being, and unhealthy or compulsive science, which promotes the defensiveness and anxiety of scientists and those they study. Maslow makes his preference clear (1966, p.48):

> In my opinion we have learned from clinical . . . experience (1) that improvement of psychological health makes the person a better knower, even a better scientist, and (2) that a very good path to improved and fuller humanness of health has been via self-knowledge, insight, and honesty with oneself.

> In effect what I am implying is that honest knowing of oneself is logically and psychologically prior to knowing the extra-psychic world.

It is important to understand that Maslow is not against science as we have known it, with its traditional emphasis on precision, exactness, and control. What he is against is the extreme, dysfunctional form of science. The following passage sets out in sharp relief another of Maslow's major themes: the dialectic between the demands of science as we have known and practiced it and recent findings concerning the conditions conducive to psychological health and growth in persons:

> These "good," "nice" scientific works—prediction, control, rigor, certainty, exactness, preciseness, neatness, orderliness, lawfulness, quantification, proof, explanation, validations, reliability, organization, etc.—are all capable of being pathologized when

pushed into the service of the safety needs, i.e., they may become primarily anxiety-avoiding and anxiety-controlling mechanisms.

All of these same mechanisms and goals are also found in the growth-motivated scientist. The difference is that they are not neuroticized. They are not compulsive, rigid, and uncontrollable, nor is anxiety produced when these rewards have to be postponed. They are not desperately needed nor are they exclusively needed. It is possible for healthy scientists to enjoy not only the beauties of precision but also the pleasures of sloppiness, casualness, and ambiguity. They are able to enjoy rationality and logic but are also able to be pleasantly crazy, wild, or emotional [1966, pp. 30-31].

The Psychological Types of C.G. Jung

Jung's psychological system is one of the very few that not only accords a place to both affect (feeling) and cognition (thinking) within a single framework, but attempts to integrate them—or at least define the barriers standing in the way of integration. We contend that the personality types of Jung provide an appropriately comprehensive framework for a typology of scientists. In particular, two dimensions of the Jungian personality system are of importance. The first dimension (informational) is the individual's preference for the kinds of input data characteristically sought in the world, either from the world external to the individual or from the inner world. The second dimension (decision-making), which is independent of and orthogonal to the first, is an individual's choice of decision-making process characteristically brought to bear upon the preferred kind of input data.

According to Jung, individuals can take in data from the world (inner or outer) either by sensation (S) or intuition (N) but not by both processes simultaneously, because as Jung defines them sensation and intuition are antithetical psychological processes. Individuals tend to develop a noticeable preference for and become more skilled at one mode of input over the other.

The sensation category consists of individuals who typically "take in" information via the senses (either from their own internal body states or the external world), who are most comfortable when attending to the details and specifics of any situation, and who prefer hard and realistic facts with regard to any matter. Sensation types are realists. They take a hard, objective stand with regard to reality. They are oriented to the "here and now." They are practical. They are concerned with what is feasible in the immediate present, not with vague plans for some unspecified future.

In contrast, the intuition category refers to those individuals who typically take in information by means of their imagination, by seeing the whole—the gestalt—of any situation. Unlike sensing types, who prefer to break any situation down into its parts and gather hard data on them, intuition types prefer to look at the whole of any situation. These individuals typically prefer the hypothetical possibilities in any situation to the actual facts. Intuitive types are idealists. They are not oriented to the immediate present or the "here and now" but prefer instead to use their imagination to take a broad, long-range view of any situation. Intuitive types prefer to concentrate on "what might be" rather than "what is." It is important that for intuitive types the hypothetical possibilities in any situation are not a substitute for reality—they *are* reality. Intuitive types feel hemmed in by fixed situations with no room to innovate. As a result they create novel situations which allow them to innovate, to experience freedom of action.

According to Jung, there are two basic ways of reaching a decision: thinking (T) and feeling (F). As in the case of sensation and intuition, these two processes are antithetical to one another, and as a result individuals tend to develop a preference for one of these two modes of decision making over the other.

Thinking is the process of reaching a decision based on impersonal, formal, or theoretical modes of reasoning. Thinking seeks to explain things in scientific, technical, and theoretical terms independent of human purposes, needs, and concerns. It is concerned with the "truth" of things, not with their moral, ethical, or aesthetic value. Thinking generalizes: given two or more people, objects, or events, it seeks to find out what they have in common in abstract, theoretical terms, not in human terms. The highest forms of thinking have been traditionally found in logic and science, where the individual is meaningful only by virtue of its membership in some theoretical system governed by a set of impersonal laws.

Feeling, in contrast, is the process of reaching a decision based on personalistic value judgments that may be unique to the particular individual. By *feeling* Jung does not mean *emotion*, for all the types are capable of emotion. Rather, by feeling Jung means a particular style of reasoning, of valuing, and of reaching a decision. Feeling types are particularly sensitive to people and to individual differences. Feeling is the psychological function which, rather than seeking to explain things in impersonal, scientific terms, seeks to empathize with and value them in human terms. Where thinking asks whether something is true or false, feeling asks whether it is good or bad, ethical or unethical, pleasing or unpleasing, likable or unlikable, to a particular individual. Feeling individuates: given two or more people, objects, or events which are presumably the same, feeling seeks to find, to draw out, to emphasize what is characteristic about each of them. Some of the highest forms of feeling are found in those ethical systems, literature, and art that stress the uniqueness and individuality of all people and demand that each person be treated as a unique "end" rather than merely as one of an infinite set of interchangeable "means" to be manipulated for some impersonal end (Kant, 1956). Feeling stresses the unique worth of each object in the universe—inanimate as well as animate.

However one takes in data (either by intuition or sensation), one may come to some conclusion about the data either by a logical, impersonal analysis (thinking) or by a personalistic process (feeling). Since these two dimensions are independent, we may combine them in four ways to get four personality types: (1) sensing-thinking (STs); (2) sensing-feeling (SFs); (3) intuition-feeling (NFs); and (4) intuition-thinking (NTs). These types possess the attributes of the particular individual characteristics they combine. Thus, the NT types contain the attributes of N and those of T. In addition, each combined type takes on a dynamic of its own which is more than the combination of the individual attributes. These interaction effects will be discussed further in later chapters.

This typology does not imply that a person is fixed in a single type for life. Indeed, one of the most important aspects of personality is the degree to which one is able to switch back and forth from one type to another. The concept of personality is dynamic, not static. It is not uncommon for a person to start out as one type in one phase of life and move increasingly towards another or even to behave as one type in one kind of situation and an entirely different type in another. This does not mean that pure types do not exist or are uncommon. Rather, the pure types are extremes. Without a clear notion of such pure or extreme types, it would be difficult to say precisely of what most people are "mixtures."

Another aspect of Jung's typology is that not only does each pure type have its extreme opposite (the extreme opposite of ST is NF; of SF, NT) but that opposite represents the unconscious, blind, or undeveloped side of the type. For example, a person who is primarily an ST spends a large proportion of life developing the ST side. The person will be able to analyze things and collect data well. However, this person will not have spent much time developing the opposite NF side, which will be unconscious and in a primitive state of development. When thrust into a situation requiring an NF response, this person will either be unable to respond or will respond only with extreme difficulty and discomfort.

Jung's system is dialectic in a number of respects. Each of the types has extreme positive and negative virtues, and the strengths of one type are the weaknesses of its opposite (and vice versa). Further, each type is defined not only by what it contains but also by what it opposes. Thus the definition of an ST cannot be accomplished solely by reference to S and T attributes but must also include reference to the attributes N and F, to which it is opposed.

The Jungian Framework as a Typology of Scientific Typologies

Figure I shows the various typologies we have discussed in this chapter plotted on the Jungian dimensions. The figure is not meant to be taken literally but figuratively. The figure is meant to suggest where the various types lie in relation to one another and their approximate locations in Jungian space. It should not be read "Technicians lie exactly two units beyond convergers," for example.

Hudson's diverger and converger types are good examples of Jung's Sensing-Thinking (ST) and Intuition-Feeling (NF) types. The converger's approach to persons, life situations, and problems is typically impersonal and analytical. The diverger typically takes a highly personal and global approach. As we have indicated, neither

Figure 1: The Jungian Framework as a Typology of Scientific Typologies

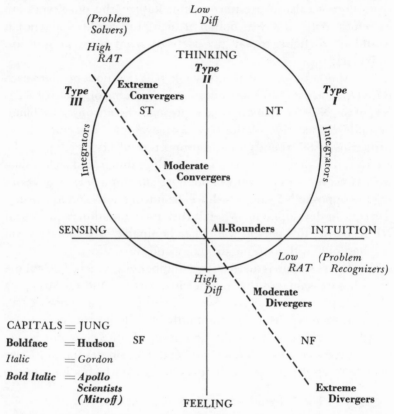

one is superior for all situations; they are merely different. At this point, we merely wish to indicate that the converger and diverger have been placed as far apart as possible in totally different quadrants of the Jungian typology and that the converger is a prime representative of the ST type and the diverger of the NF type.

The placement of Gordon and Morse's types is complicated by the alignment of their dimensions with that of Jung's. While it is clear that differentiation relates to the thinking-feeling dimension, we have resisted the temptation to align it with the whole T-F continuum for a number of reasons. Basically, differentiation does not seem to tap the entire Jungian dimension of thinking-feeling. It is clear that high differentiators, by virtue of their view of persons, objects, and events as distinct entities, are moving down into the realm of feeling. The question is how far down into the realm of feeling is high differentiation located. Although we lack sufficient data to be definitive, there is evidence (McClelland, 1970) that points to the fact that high differentiation cannot be placed further than the dividing line between feeling and thinking. This evidence suggests that feeling is the psychological function that is the most conspicuously underdeveloped in modern science. Thus, compared with pure low differentiators, high differentiators stand out as extreme feeling types, but in comparison with what Jung means by feeling, high differentiators are not pure feeling types.

Of all the dimensions, Gordon's RAT is the hardest to place. An initial temptation is to align High RAT with Intuition and Low RAT with Sensing. However, High RAT is not measuring Intuition as Jung defines it but the ability to solve a prearranged puzzle or well-defined problem in the Kuhnian sense. The situation is even more complicated by the interaction effect between the RAT and differentiation scales. Indeed, extensive personal conversations with Gordon and his colleagues revealed that the Problem Solver (High RAT, Low Differentiation) is a version of the ST personality type and the Problem Recognizer (Low RAT, High Differentiation) is a version of NF. Where does this leave the Technician and the Integrator? If we interpret the RAT as a performance measure, as Gordon and his colleagues do, then the Technician can also be conceived of as an ST (Low RAT, Low Differentiation)—although a poorly functioning one. (Not all ST's are the same just as not all logicians are of the same caliber.) ST defines a broad style, not a single way of behaving or of equal performance. While the Technician is an ST in orientation, he is not of the same level of skills and performance as the Problem Solver. In other words, there is no one-to-one alignment of both scales on the Jungian ones but a complex interaction. This is perhaps best seen by the placement of the Integrator (High RAT, High Differentiation), who is best described by a rotating curve that dips into all of the Jungian quadrants, although not equally in distance. The Integrator is defined by ability to recognize a problem and to solve it, and this calls for ability to tap into all of Jung's dimensions.

Regarding the Mitroff typology, we see the Type III scientist in the neighborhood of the Problem Solver and Extreme Con-

verger. By virtue of the defintion of the Type II scientist and the
firm data we possess on the alignment of the Type I, II, and III
scientists in relationship to one another (Mitroff, 1976), we are
confident about the placement of these scientists on the Jungian
typology. (See Mitroff's 1974b for details.)

We feel that the Jungian typology is capable of providing a
sufficiently comprehensive framework to compare the various
typologies as well as providing us with some other important benefits. By plotting some of the typologies currently available we not
only have an opportunity to see where they fall on the Jungian
typology but also where there are gaps in our current thinking
regarding science. While there exists some uncertainty regarding
the exact placement of some of the types, in particular Gordon and
Morse's, we do not believe that it is merely an artifact of our analysis
that intuition-feeling (NF) and sensation-feeling (SF) types are the
least represented or acknowledged in current typologies of science.
There is some rather dramatic evidence that feeling is the
psychological function historically and currently least represented
in science, especially in the physical sciences (McClelland, 1970).
This is not to say that feeling is altogether absent. Indeed, the
strong emergence of feeling is characteristic of the newly developing approaches in the social sciences. Any typology that did not
allow for the representation of this important psychological dimension would be greatly flawed in our opinion. Hudson, Jung, and
Maslow, in particular, offer us strong clues to the origin and function of impersonality in science and strong grounds for challenging
this established, often unchallenged basis. There are not only
strong Apollonian and Dionysion forces evaluating science from
the outside (Holton, 1974); there are equally strong opposing
forces operating within science.

Based upon the general clustering of the various types of
scientists on the Jungian matrix (see Figure 1) and taking into
consideration the affective and cognitive qualities inherent in each
of these types, we have devised descriptive names for each of the
four Jungian quadrants. These four classifications comprise our
own typology, which will be examined in detail in Chapters Three
through Six. The four approaches represented in the four Jungian
quadrants are: (1) the Analytical Scientist (AS—Jung's ST quad-

rant); (2) the Conceptual Theorist (CT—Jung's NT quadrant); (3) the Conceptual Humanist (CH—Jung's NF quadrant); and (4) the Particular Humanist (PH—Jung's SF quadrant).

Although the Jungian typology has by now received considerable empirical testing and validation via accepted scientific procedures (Myers-Briggs, 1962) (the ST or the Analytic Scientific approach), we realize that like all personality typologies the validation has not been perfect, and perhaps never will be. In fact there are conflicting views on the usefulness of typologies at all. But however primitive our knowledge of the psychology of scientists, we ignore this psychology only at our own peril. Every view of science, no matter how removed it seems from the realm of everyday practice, makes some important assumptions about the psychology of the scientist. For example, Popper's (1965, 1970) views presuppose a mind both able and predisposed to act as a falsificationist. It is important to know whether scientists can act as such, particularly as there is evidence that even the best scientists do not. Mahoney (1976) has recently completed a series of clever experiments showing that scientists are not prone to attempt to falsify their hypotheses but rather attempt to verify or confirm them. When compared with a sample of ministers, scientists were less prone to questioning their own hypotheses. This raises an interesting question: if falsification is a desirable aim of science, then what special psychological training is necessary to enable scientists to do this? Mere logical or philosophical exhortations seem unlikely to produce the desired result.

Perhaps it is best to acknowledge that we are inevitably thrust into the middle of a circle. We must explicitly adopt a psychology of science in order to fashion a new methodology of social science, and yet the validation of the psychology with which we have chosen to begin presupposes, if only in part, the development of this new methodology. In the remainder of this book, particularly the concluding chapters, we shall have to return and come to grips with this issue. We shall postpone it for now until we have examined each of our four main types for their implications for the methodology of the social sciences.

THREE

The Analytic Scientist

Science rejects the indeterminate.

* * *

When faced by complex questions, physiologists and physicians, as well as physicists and chemists, should divide the total problem into simpler and simpler and more and more clearly defined partial problems. They will thus reduce phenomena to their simplest possible material conditions and make application of the experimental method easier and more certain.

Claude Bernard (1957, pp. 55, 72)

In this chapter we describe the first of the four methodologies that are the object of this book. We hope to demonstrate that the characteristics of the Analytic Scientist are not random, separate manifestations of different phenomena but common manifestations of a single phenomenon. More specifically, we hope to demonstrate that the methodology which we identify as characteristic of the Analytic Scientist is the outer manifestation of the inner psychological attitude of the ST (sensing-thinking) quadrant of the Jungian typology.

The outlook of the Analytic Scientist is representative of a very particular world view which embodies, among other things, a style of conducting inquiry, a set of sociological norms regarding the institutional aims of science, a general scientific ideology, and a preferred logic (that is, a *formal* style of reasoning).

The outlook of the Analytic Scientist (AS) is characterized by a diverse set of attributes, some of which are displayed in Table 1. These characteristics can be easily understood once it is appreciated that the AS's basic drive is toward certainty and the corresponding desire to eliminate or avoid uncertainty as much as possible in regard to knowledge and human affairs in general. When the need for certainty threatens to drive out and suppress all the other concerns of inquiry, we speak of an extreme or unhealthy AS attitude. When certainty is sought only when appropriate to the inquiry at hand and not insisted upon for all inquiries all the time, we speak of a more moderate or healthy AS attitude. It is not always easy to differentiate between the more extreme and more moderate forms of AS because both embody basically the same set of attributes in Table 1. Moderate ASs, however, to quote Maslow, "are not neuroticized. They are not compulsive, rigid, and uncontrollable" (1966, p. 30).

To show how the drive for certainty links up with the other attributes, consider, for example, three important characteristics of the AS: precision, accuracy, and reliability. It is a basic tenet of the AS's approach that precision, accuracy, and reliability necessarily serve the ultimate aim of scientific knowledge, which is unambiguous theoretical or empirical knowledge. Put in the form of a syllogism, the argument runs as follows: "To know" is to be certain about something. Certainty is defined by the ability to "phrase" or enumerate the components of an object, event, person, or situation in a precise, accurate, and reliable fashion. Therefore, knowledge is synonymous with precision, accuracy, and reliability. Any endeavor that cannot be subjected to this formula or line of reasoning is either suppressed, devalued, or set aside as not worth knowing or capable of being known.

Consider, for example, one of the most important aspects of the AS's world view, the belief in the value-free nature of science. The contention is that science only uncovers impersonal facts upon which disinterested theories are erected. These theories are then tested (or ought to be) independent of the shifting desires of human interests and biases. A crisper way of putting this is that

Table 1. Characteristics of the Analytic Scientist

	Evaluative categories	Attributed characteristics
External relations	Status of science as a special field of knowledge in relation to other fields	Occupies a privileged and a preferred position: value-free, apolitical, cumulative, progressive, disinterested, clearly separable from other fields, clear lines of demarcation, autonomous, independent, strict hierarchical ordering of scientific fields from precise to less precise fields
Internal properties	A. Nature of scientific knowledge	Impersonal, value-free, disinterested, precise, reliable, accurate, valid, reductionistic, causal, apolitical, cumulative, progressive, clear standards for judgment, realistic, antimystical, unambiguous, exact
	B. Guarantors of scientific knowledge	Consensus, agreement, reliability, external validity, rigor, controlled nature of inquiry, maintenance of distance between scientist and objects studied
	C. Ultimate aims of science	Precise, unambiguous, theoretical and empirical knowledge for their own (disinterested) sake
	D. Preferred logic	Aristotelian, strict classical logic, nondialectical and indeterminate
	E. Preferred sociological norms (ideology)	Classical norms of science: CUDOS
	F. Preferred mode of inquiry	Controlled inquiry as embodied in the classic concept of the experiment
	G. Properties of the scientist	Disinterested, unbiased, impersonal, precise, expert, specialist, skeptical, exact, methodical

knowledge is separable from values. Upon deeper examination, this thesis is found seriously wanting (Churchman, 1961). However, at this point we merely wish to state that the belief in the value-free nature of scientific inquiry is one of the central tenets in the AS's world view. Any philosophical arguments to the contrary are unlikely to change the AS's belief in this fundamental tenet, for they would first have to be expressed in the AS's language. This "self-sealing" of the AS's world view serves to insulate and protect the value-free doctrine from challenge.

Consider the following: While it is clear to the reflective psychologist that the belief in a value-free science partially derives from that aspect of the AS's constitution which is averse to value judgments, it is clear that the belief also derives from the failure of value judgments to command the kind of universal assent which scientific statements seem to command. Here again, certainty enters in. In principle, given the same conditions, different observers can agree that they have observed the same thing. Indeed, agreement or consensus is so important to this form of science that it is turned around as an epistemic guarantor of the validity of a scientific observation: a scientific observation is judged valid, reliable, or certain if two or more "competent" observers in different places at different times can agree on what they have observed. According to Norman Campbell "science is the study of those judgments concerning which universal agreement can be reached" (1952, p. 27). This definition is plagued by enumerable difficulties; such as what is meant by the terms *judgment, universal, agreement,* and *study.* Further, it is not at all clear that a science founded on *disagreement* is meaningless or impossible (Churchman, 1961, 1971). In fact, we shall later consider positions diametrically opposed to Campbell's; the basic principle of these positions is that social science is the study of judgments that provoke disagreement between different groups of people. For now, however, we merely wish to note that agreement or consensus forms one of the epistemic cornerstones of the AS's approach.

This agreement seems fundamentally lacking with regard to value issues. People consistently disagree on what they value, not to mention what they ought to value (Churchman, 1961). One of the main points of Chapter Two was that different psychological types not only value different things but experience the same things within very different value systems. If agreement is used as a principal criterion for the establishment of valid knowledge—as is the AS's world view—then a number of implications follow. One is that value statements are necessarily ambiguous, and since knowledge and certainty are linked together in the AS's system, value statements do not represent knowledge at all. They are merely "meaningless" emotive statements. The most far reaching implication of this line of reasoning is that there simply cannot be a science of values.

Consensus and certainty also enter into the AS's world view in a number of subtle ways. What sets science apart from other fields is not merely that science obtains a wide consensus of opinion—a consensus lacking in such fields as philosophy, morals, and art—but that science alone is truly capable of making clear progress and in this sense is superior as a method of obtaining knowledge. Consider the following statements by Ziman and by Sarton.

> As so often said, science cannot tell us what *ought* to be done; it can only chart the consequences of what *might* be done.
>
> Normative and moral principles cannot, by definition, be embraced in a consensus; to assert that one *ought* to do so and so is to admit that some people, at least, will not freely recognize the absolute necessity of not doing otherwise. Legal principles and norms are neither external nor universal; they are attached to the local, ephemeral situation of this country here and now; their arbitrariness can never be mended by any amount of further logical manipulation [Ziman, 1968, p. 15].

> Scientific activity is the only one which is obviously and undoubtedly cumulative and progressive. . . . The fact is there cannot be any continuous progress in art or in literature. When one reads the history of science one has the exhilarating feeling of climbing a big mountain. The history of art gives one an altogether different impression.
>
> In almost every case wherever there is progress or a possibility of progress, this is due to science and its applications. I would

never claim that science is more important than art, morality, or religion, but it is more fundamental, for progress in any direction is always subordinated to some form or other of scientific progress [Sarton, 1962, p. 45].

We do not contend that Sarton is himself an Analytic Scientist but rather that his statements agree with what we identify as characteristic of the AS outlook.

The progressive aspect of science can be taken to an unhealthy extreme if, in its quest for certainty, the "progress" must always end in the total elimination of doubt. John Dewey, who was not particularly sympathetic with the AS's outlook, characterized this approach as an "obsessive quest for certainty": "any philosophy that in its quest for certainty ignores the reality of the uncertain in the ongoing processes of nature denies the conditions out of which it arises. The attempt to include all that is doubtful within the fixed grasp of that which is theoretically certain is committed to insincerity and evasion, and in consequence will have the stigmatic of internal contradiction. Every such philosophy is marked at some point by a division of its subject matter into the truly real and the merely apparent, a subject and an object, a physical and a mental, an ideal and an actual, that have nothing to do with one another, save some mode which is so mysterious as to create an unsoluble problem" (1960, p. 244).

Preferred Style of Inquiry

To understand fully the Analytic Scientist's viewpoint, it is necessary to study the details of the AS's methodology. A turning point in the history of research methodology was the publication of J. S. Mill's *A System of Logic* (1872). The importance of Mill's book is that it not only outlined a method whereby an experimenter could systematically discover whether two events were causally connected but also set the foundation for modern research methods founded on statistical reasoning. Specifically, Mill's work laid the foundation for the role of analysis of variance (ANOVA) in modern experimental design.

Mill's principles are important for our purposes because they embody the tenets of the AS's approach. Mill's principles are expressed in various canons which the experimenter is enjoined to follow in order to discover whether two events, X and Y, are causally connected.

The first principle is known as the Method of Agreement or Canon I. Suppose an experimenter has observed that two events X and Y seem to be connected such that whenever X is present, Y follows. Since two events rarely, if ever, occur in isolation, other events, A, B, C, and so forth, will inevitably occur along with X in order for Y to occur. That is, A, B, and C, along with X, are hypothesized as the joint causes of the effect Y. To establish whether X is indeed one of the causes of Y, the experimenter is instructed to set up two conditions:

$$\text{X, A, B, C} \longrightarrow \text{Y} \tag{1}$$
$$\text{X, } \overline{\text{A}}, \overline{\text{B}}, \overline{\text{C}} \longrightarrow \text{Y} \tag{2}$$

The first condition instructs the experimenter (E) to observe whether Y follows when X, A, B, and C are present. The second condition instructs E to observe whether Y still follows when X is present but A, B, C are *not* present (represented by $\overline{\text{A}}, \overline{\text{B}}, \overline{\text{C}}$). If Y still occurs when $\overline{\text{A}}, \overline{\text{B}}, \overline{\text{C}}$, then X is said to be *sufficient* for the occurrence of Y.

Canon II is known as the Method of Difference. It is also expressed in two experimental conditions:

$$\text{X, A, B, C} \longrightarrow \text{Y} \tag{1'}$$
$$\overline{\text{X}}, \text{A, B, C} \longrightarrow \overline{\text{Y}} \tag{2'}$$

That is, E is instructed to observe whether Y follows given the prior presence of X and whether Y does *not* follow ($\overline{\text{Y}}$) given the absence of X ($\overline{\text{X}}$). If so, then X is said to be *necessary* for the occurrence of Y.

The third canon is known as the Method of Joint Occurrence and is illustrated as follows:

$$\text{X, A, B, C} \longrightarrow \text{Y} \tag{1''}$$
$$\text{X, } \overline{\text{A}}, \overline{\text{B}}, \overline{\text{C}} \longrightarrow \text{Y} \tag{2''}$$
$$\overline{\text{X}}, \text{A, B, C} \longrightarrow \overline{\text{Y}} \tag{3''}$$

That is E is instructed to combine Canons I and II in order to establish whether X is both necessary and sufficient for the occurrence of Y.*

A number of fundamental difficulties with Mill's canons are basic to our discussion. Mill thought he was formulating a method whereby one could discover by experimental or observational means whether two events, X and Y, were causally related. Contrary to Mill's expectations, however, the canons presuppose that we already know (via some prior means) the very things we are supposed to discover via the canons. In other words, Mill's canons are means by which we test what we have discovered by other means.

Consider the basic schema X, A, B, C $\longrightarrow$ Y, which is inherent in the canons. No amount of repeated application of this schema will allow us to discover which particular factors X, A, B, C, Y to put into this schema in the first place. Application of the schema presupposes that we already know what we wish to subject to the schema. All the schema says is that given this particular array of X, A, B, C, and Y, one can test whether X and Y stand in a causal relationship to one another. But the strong claim Mill made for his canons was that by means of these canons alone the dutiful experimenter was supposed to be able to discover empirically causal relationships. An even more fundamental difficulty is that the canons assume that nature can be partitioned into causes and effects—into clear and distinct factors X, A, B, C, Y, and so on. However, we cannot validate this assumption through application of the canons, because application itself requires this assumption. The point is a Kantian one: Unless we are first willing to posit the metaphysical principle that the world is capable of being partitioned into separate factors (some labeled causes, others effects), we cannot engage in empirical observations. We cannot validate a metaphysical prin-

*There are two other canons which we shall not bother to discuss; one is essentially a variation of the first canon and the other—known as Method of Concomitant Variations—is not essential to our discussion. The latter canon, although it was formulated by Mill in a purely qualitative form, later became the basis for modern correlational analysis, that is, whether two events X and Y are correlated with one another as measured by, for example, the Pearson product-moment coefficient.

ciple by observations which are themselves only made possible through prior assumption of the metaphysicial principle itself.

The point is not just philosophical but psychological and cultural as well. The cultural anthropologist Edmund Leach (1973) has presented a fascinating argument that it is the social concept of "taboo" that allows us to fashion discrete entities. The world of objects is originally a continuum where object A slides into B, but there is a human need for organization that separates them from one another. "Our uninhibited (untrained) perception recognizes a continuum . . . . We are taught that the world consists of "things" distinguished by names; therefore we have to train our perception to recognize a discontinuous environment. We achieve this . . . trained perception by means of a simultaneous use of language and taboo. Language gives us the names to distinguish the things; taboo inhibits the recognition of those parts of the continuum which separate the things" (1973, p. 47). Leach suggests that the separation of the factors A,B, and so forth, from one another is not entirely a rational process but one that has deep, underlying psychological and social overtones. In a word, it is psychologically dangerous for us to have a world where A and B are not distinct from one another. So via unconscious processes such as taboo and repression, we invent a world of discrete, distinct entities.

We do not mean to imply that Mill's canons are not valuable or did not represent a significant advance in experimental methodology. Rather we wish to point out that instead of being purely empirical principles, the canons are one way of representing the metaphysical postulates of the AS's world view—they represent the projection of the AS's psyche onto the world. In the words of the distinguished nineteenth century physiologist, Claude Bernard, "With the help of experiment, we analyze, we disassociate these phenomena, in order to reduce them to more and more simple relations and conditions. In two ways we try to lay hold on scientific truth, that is, find the law that shall give us the key to all variations of the phenomena. Thus, experimental analysis is our only means of going in search of truth in the natural sciences, and the absolute determinism of phenomena, of which we are conscious *a priori,* is the only criterion or principle which directs and supports us" (1957, p. 54).

In addition to the aforementioned philosophical difficulties, there are some technical difficulties as well with Mill's canons. Consider again Canon I, the Method of Agreement:

$$X, A, B, C \longrightarrow Y \tag{1}$$
$$X, \overline{A}, \overline{B}, \overline{C} \longrightarrow Y \tag{2}$$

In their original form, these two experimental conditions do not adequately establish the sufficiency of X for Y. In addition to these two conditions, we would need to know whether the presence of X alone under every conceivable condition of the presence or absence of A, B, and C results in the occurrence of Y; that is, we would need to test for the following eight conditions:

$$X, A, B, C, \longrightarrow Y \tag{1}$$
$$X, \overline{A}, \overline{B}, \overline{C}, \longrightarrow Y \tag{2}$$
$$X, \overline{A}, B, C, \longrightarrow Y \tag{3}$$
$$X, A, \overline{B}, C, \longrightarrow Y \tag{4}$$
$$X, A, B, \overline{C} \longrightarrow Y \tag{5}$$
$$X, \overline{A}, \overline{B}, C \longrightarrow Y \tag{6}$$
$$X, \overline{A}, B, \overline{C} \longrightarrow Y \tag{7}$$
$$X, A, \overline{B}, \overline{C} \longrightarrow Y \tag{8}$$

Canon I assumes that there are no interactions between A, B, and C, either among themselves or between them and X and Y. As we know from modern ANOVA methods, we cannot automatically make such an assumption. In addition, conditions (1) through (8) above assume that only the factors X, A, B, and C are involved in the occurrence of Y. It may not be the occurrence of these alone that cause Y but some other factor D of which we are unaware. The method presupposes our prior knowledge of a finite set of factors. These same difficulties apply to each of the remaining canons as well.

We have devoted this much attention to Mill both because he is the precursor of modern experimental methods and because the form of the canons helps explain the AS's concern with precision, accuracy, control, reliability, reproducibility of results, and so forth. Consider again the basic schema X, A, B, C $\longrightarrow$ Y. If this is conceived of as a basic and valid schema for the representation and explication of nature, then an experimenter must first of all be able to enumerate precisely, reliably, and accurately the potential factors X, A, B, C entering into the causation of Y and then be able to determine precisely, reliably, and accurately the degree to which each factor contributes to the causation of Y.

Analysis of variance (ANOVA) procedures are the latest in a series of powerful techniques designed to answer the preceding concerns. In ANOVA terms, the extremely simple schema X, A$\longrightarrow$Y can be expressed as follows:

		a_1	a_2	$\cdots$	a_j	$\cdots$	a_m
	x_1	y_{11}	y_{12}	$\cdots$	y_{1j}	$\cdots$	y_{1m}
	x_2	y_{21}	y_{22}	$\cdots$	y_{2j}	$\cdots$	y_{2m}
		$\vdots$	$\vdots$	$\cdots$	$\vdots$	$\cdots$	$\vdots$
X	x_i	y_{i1}	y_{i2}	$\cdots$	y_{ij}	$\cdots$	y_{im}
		$\vdots$	$\vdots$	$\cdots$	$\vdots$	$\cdots$	$\vdots$
	x_ℓ	$y_{\ell 1}$	$y_{\ell 2}$	$\cdots$	$y_{\ell j}$	$\cdots$	$y_{\ell m}$

(Header spanning columns: **A**)

Modern ANOVA represents a considerable expansion and sophistication of Mill's canons. Instead of a potential causative factor X or A being either strictly present (X, A) or absent ($\overline{X}$, $\overline{A}$), ANOVA methods allow one to consider various degrees of the presence of a factor. In the matrix, x_1 through x_ℓ represent ℓ distinctly different levels of the presence of factor X; a_1 through a_m represent m distinct levels of factor A. ANOVA allows one to determine the extent to which changes in the levels of X and A affect the degree of occurrence of Y. In more precise terms, it allows one to answer the following question: Are changes in X and A accompanied by statistically significant changes in Y?

It is clear why precision is so important: Unless we can first specify the distinct levels of X and A in an unambiguous fashion, we cannot determine precisely the extent to which any particular level of X (say x_i) and A (a_j) contribute to Y (y_{ij}). Further, if factors X and A are not distinct—if they overlap—then we cannot determine precisely which of the two factors X and A contributes to the presence of Y—there will be a "confounding of effects."

This problem of confounding is reflected in one of the most sophisticated treatments of experimental method to appear to date, the pioneering work of Campbell and Stanley (1969). In their terms the simplest possible schema, $X \longrightarrow Y$, reads as follows:

$$O_1 \; X \; O_2 \tag{9}$$

$$O_3 \; \overline{X} \; O_4 \tag{10}$$

At a given time, t_1, we take a set of observations O_1 on the behavior of attitudes of an individual or group of individuals. Next, we administer some treatment or condition X to the individual or group to see if X has produced a change (O_2) in the original condition O_1. In this schema, X is called the causative agent or experimental treatment. Y in this schema is represented by the difference $O_2 - O_1$. Equation(10) determines whether the absence of X ($\overline{X}$) causes no change between O_4 and O_3; $\overline{Y} = \phi = O_4 - O_3$ or $O_4 = O_3$, no change. Notice that equations (9) and (10) represent Mill's second canon; at best, they establish the necessity of X for Y, not sufficiency.

The problem of confounding plays a central role in the schema of Campbell and Stanley. They have worked out an elaborate system with two classes of categories for controlling for the possible effects of confounding. The first class in concerned with "threats to internal validity" and the second with "threats to external validity." *"Internal validity* is the basic minimum without which any experiment is uninterpretable: Did in fact the experimental treatments [the X] make a difference in this specific experimental instance? *External validity* asks the question of *generalizability:* To what populations, settings, variables can this effect be generalized? Both types of criteria are obviously important, even though they are frequently at odds in that features increasing one may jeopardize the other" (Campbell and Stanley, 1969, p. 5). Internal validity asks whether there are factors other than X in equation (9) causing a difference (O_2-O_1) in Y. If there are such factors, then unless we control for their potential confounding influence, we will wrongly conclude that it was X that produced a difference between O_2 and O_1 when in fact it was some other factor.

Campbell and Stanley list eight influences that an experimenter should attempt to control under internal validity and four under external validity. Since our purpose is to illustrate the general nature of these influences and not to discuss each one in detail, we shall merely discuss seven influences of internal validity: history, maturation, testing, instrumentation, statistical regression, differential selection biases, and experimental mortality.

History refers to all those influences occurring in the environment external to the experiment such that, if they are not controlled for, they will produce a change in $O_2 - O_1$ that may or may not be related to that produced by X alone. Since the whole point of doing an experiment is to find out precisely those changes due to X and X alone, unless one controls for history, the experiment will be worthless. Changes in the quantity $(O_2 - O_1)$ or in just O_2 alone due to X will be confounded with changes due to history. To give an example, suppose we are interested in measuring the differences in attitude towards a certain country before (O_1) and after (O_2) a group of individuals is exposed to a series of lectures (X) on the country. If, during the time between the measurement of initial (O_1) and final (O_2) attitudes, an international incident (such as war) occurs involving the country, then a change in $O_2 - O_1$ might not be caused by X but rather by the fact of war breaking out. Thus,.it could be both X and the international incident producing change in $O_2 - O_1$.

Maturation refers to all those changes occurring within the individuals or subjects (Ss) in an experiment. If the time span of an experiment is long, then the change $(O_2 - O_1)$ will not be due solely to X but to the normal change occurring over time within the Ss, such as growth and development of attitudes.

Testing refers to the effects of an initial test or observation (O_1) on subsequent test scores or observations (O_2). Changes in this case $(O_2 - O_1)$ may again be due not to X but to the fact that taking the first test sensitized the Ss to the items and issues on the test so that they are reacting to it and not to X. For example, tests that measure prejudice sometimes contain racial and ethnic slurs that precipitate the very prejudice they are trying to measure. The subjects are highly reactive to the measuring instrument itself as well as to the phenomenon being tested.

Instrumentation refers to the fact that between O_2 and O_1 the instrument designed to measure (observations) can change. If this occurs, there will be an indicated difference between O_2 and O_1 that may be due entirely to differences in the measuring instrument.

Statistical regression and *differential selection* biases are similar enough for our purposes to warrant a single discussion. These biases occur when we select for an experiment Ss whose scores on initial test O_1 are either very high or very low. If there is a natural tendency over time for extreme scores to regress toward the mean of a population, then a change (O_2-O_1) will be observed that is due largely to regression effects and not to X.

Experimental mortality occurs when Ss of a particular type drop out of an experiment due to the nature of the experiment, resulting in change O_2-O_1. For example, suppose at the beginning of an experiment designed to measure racial attitudes, the more "liberal" Ss are so offended by the nature of the tests that they drop out. In this case the change O_2-O_1 may be due more to this than to X alone.

The importance of the preceding concepts is that they serve as guides in the selection of an appropriate design for experimental research—they are both prescriptive and evaluative criteria in experimental design. As such, they represent the AS's meta-criteria for the conduct of one of his preferred inquiry, the controlled experiment. Since they were first codified by Campbell and Stanley, these criteria have been widely acclaimed as the proper criteria for the design and evaluation of experimental inquiry in the social sciences, and the controlled experiment has been proclaimed the preferred, if not superior, mode of obtaining knowledge. Campbell and Stanley are committed to the experiment "as the only means for settling disputes regarding educational practice, as the only way of verifying educational improvements and as the only way of establishing a cumulative tradition in which improvements can be introduced without the danger of a faddish discard of old wisdom in favor of inferior novelties" (1969, p. 2).

Two questions arise from this claim: (1) Do the preceding criteria strongly influence, if not dictate, the selection and evaluation of a particular experimental design? That is, does the adoption of this particular set of criteria commit us to the acceptance of certain kinds of designs and the rejection of others? (2) Does this particular set exhaust all the desirable criteria that one could associate with an inquiry.—even an experimental inquiry in the social sciences? The answer to the first question is "yes"; the answer to the second is "no."

Consider one of the first designs which Campbell and Stanley evaluate—the "one-shot case study." It is represented by the schema $X \rightarrow O$. We administer a treatment (X) to an individual or group of individuals and observe the resultant effects (O). Campbell and Stanley (1969) and Rossi (1972) point out that in terms of their criteria "such studies have such a total absence of control as to be of almost no scientific value. . . . Basic to scientific evidence . . . is the process of comparison, of recording differences, or of contrast. Any appearance of absolute knowledge, or intrinsic knowledge about singular isolated objects, is found to be illusory upon analysis. Securing scientific evidence involves making at least one comparison" (Campbell and Stanley, 1969, p. 6). We would have to collect a minimum set of observations O_1 prior to the administration of X, followed by O_2, or $X \rightarrow Y = O_2 - O_1$. To make this design even stronger—to approach what Campbell and Stanley call the class of "true" experimental designs—we would have to include the control group design $\overline{X} \rightarrow \overline{Y} = O_4 - O_3 = \phi$ in order to establish the necessity of X for Y and perhaps as many as three different types of control group designs (along with a fourth as an experimental treatment design) to account for the different threats to internal and external validity. The point is that given the criteria of Campbell and Stanley, certain designs will be preferred over others. Would the same designs be preferred using other criteria? This leads us to the more basic question of whether there are indeed other criteria.

Along with widespread acclaim and acceptance of Campbell and Stanley's ideas regarding experimental design, there has also been some sharp criticism. A number of social scientists have spoken out regarding the limitations of the controlled experiment (Argyris, 1973). However, it is interesting that no critics have attacked the issue at its root: the formal codification of alternate criteria for the evaluation of experimental designs. This is partly because some forceful critics of the experimental design tradition represent other traditions which do not necessarily value the formal elucidation of their own position. Since we do not believe that the formal exposition of a tradition is necessarily inconsistent with that tradition, when we come to these other traditions in later chapters, we shall attempt to express systematically their criteria for the conduct of an inquiry. We contend that there are indeed other sets of criteria and that the selection of any particular experimental design is not automatic but is a function of one's world view as well as a response to particular technical requirements.

Preferred Sociological Norms (Ideology)

The sociological properties that the AS attributes to the institutional structure of science follow from that same world view that shapes the preferred mode of inquiry. Mitroff (1974a, 1974b) has argued that the norms that are expressive of the AS's institutional outlook are deeply rooted in the impersonal structure of science. Given what has preceded us thus far, we now argue that the AS's norms are deeply rooted in his characterization of science in impersonal terms. Whether science is or is not an impersonal mechanism for the production of knowledge is open to debate; it is as much a function of the AS's outlook as it is of the institution of science itself.

Mitroff (1974a, 1974b) has also argued that there is a particular set of norms which are most expressive of the impersonal structure of science. These norms have been formalized and codified by Robert K. Merton (1968) and his colleagues and students (Barber, 1952; Storer, 1966). In recent years these norms have come under sharp scrutiny and criticism (see Barnes and Dolby, 1970; King, 1971; Mitroff, 1974a, 1974b; Mulkay, 1969), but they still represent the best exposition of the norms which are indicative of the AS's outlook. Whether these norms are literally part of the social system of science is somewhat beside the point. Indeed, we have grave reservations about the applicability and existence of every single one of these norms, but we believe they are expressive of a particular way of viewing science. While we would not label Merton and his followers as ASs themselves, we do believe that they have codified the norms of the AS outlook just as the critics of these norms (including ourselves) have codified the norms of the other outlooks we will discuss in later chapters.

Since these norms have received such extensive treatment in the literature, we need not discuss them in detail. Our main purpose here is to illustrate how they form a natural part of the AS's outlook. These norms can be conveniently recalled by a simple acronym, CUDOS—*Communism, Universalism, Disinterestedness,* and *Organized Skepticism.*

Communism does not refer to a political philosophy; indeed, ASs strongly contend that since science must be value free, it must also be free from political considerations. A strong value judgment is operating here: scientific statements *ought* to be value free. If ASs adopt any political attitude at all, it is one of apoliticism or even antipoliticism. They believe that one should not be a partisan advocate either for a political cause or for a favored scientific theory or issue—or at least that any political advocacy should be clearly separate from one's beliefs and actions as a scientist.

Communism in this context refers to the notion that scientific knowledge is common property open to all qualified scientists. It refers to the open, unrestricted, and free exchange of scientific ideas and information. Under this concept, secrecy, withholding, or hoarding of special information is antithetical to the very nature of the scientific enterprise. There is an implied categorical imperative operating that if all scientists were to practice secrecy, then science would cease to exist because the cumulative nature of science would be seriously compromised. Instead of being able to build upon the efforts of colleagues, each scientist would be forced to re-create anew the knowledge base of science.

Universalism means that scientific knowledge is (or should be) independent of the personality of the individual scientist. The claims of a scientific proposition should be evaluated solely on the merits of the proposition itself without regard to who is proposing it. The claims of a young, unknown scientist deserve as much impartial examination as those of an older, established scientist. (It has been argued that this ideal is not always the case; see Hensler, 1976; Mitroff and Chubin, 1978.)

Disinterestedness does not mean that scientists are disinterested observers or participants in the "game" of nature—if anything, they are partisan advocates of the cause of science. Rather, disinterestedness as a sociological norm means that while a scientist receives credit for a discovery, he or she is not expected to reap personal monetary gain from the discovery. Scientific ideas do not belong to individual scientists but to the community as a whole. They are community property, not individual. As Sarton (1962, pp. 116–117) says, "You understand, entire surrender of self (before the facts): that is what I call disinterestedness; nothing less. One cannot help feeling that any such disinterested effort must increase the sum of good will in the world."

Finally, *organized skepticism* refers to the fact that scientists are expected to adopt a critical attitude toward the ideas of their colleagues and themselves. Science is founded upon scientists' criticism of one another's ideas. We are entitled to claim confirmation of a scientific idea only if it keeps proving its worth after repeated efforts to falsify it, if even then.

These, briefly, are the norms of the AS. Some sociologists have felt that scientists adhere to these norms in principle (if not always in practice) not because scientists are superior people but because "scientists clearly understand that it is in their best interests to follow these principles" (Storer, 1966). Science, as opposed to other professions, has been able to make progress because of its strict adherence to these principles. "The experimental method is characterized by being dependent only on itself, because it includes within itself its criterion—experience. It recognizes no authority other than that of facts and is free from personal authority" (Bernard, 1957, p. 40).

Preferred Logic

Logic has been called the caretaker of man's reason. We turn now to the particular kind of caretaker in which the AS invests faith—that is, the AS's conception of logic and the place accorded to logic in the AS's overall scheme of inquiry. In particular this relates to (1) certain "fundamental logical laws," (2) classical or two-truth logic, and (3) logic as a special or preferred science in itself.

Two principles are basic to the AS's conception of logic—so basic that they have often been taken as fundamental laws of thought, fundamental characteristics of the structure of reality itself, or both. Anyone consciously violating these principles is considered mistaken, irrational, or simply incapable of understanding what it means to reason in accordance with valid principles. The two principles, which are foundations of Aristotelian logic, are: (1) The Law of Contradiction—no proposition can be both true and false at the same time; and (2) The Law of the Excluded Middle— every proposition is either true or false. In symbolic terms, these can be expressed as: (1) Law of Contradiction— $\sim$ (p and $\sim$ p); (2) Law of Excluded Middle—(p or $\sim$ p), where $\sim$ is to be read "not." Thus, (1) it is not the case that p and not-p are or can both be true at the same time and (2) either p or not-p is true, but not both simultaneously.

To see how important these principles are, we consider another fundamental principle of logic, the "law of implication" (also known as the "constructive hypothetical syllogism" or *modus ponens*). If a proposition p is true, then by hypothesis q is true (p implies q); but p is in fact true; hence q is true. In symbols this can be expressed:

$$\begin{array}{ll} \text{If p, then q} & p \longrightarrow q \\ \underline{\text{But p is true}} & \underline{p} \\ \text{Therefore, q} \quad \text{or} \quad \text{Therefore, q} \\ \text{is true} \end{array}$$

Even more compactly, we can write $[(p \longrightarrow q) \text{ and } p] \longrightarrow q$. Further, it is shown in elementary logic texts that $p \longrightarrow q$ can be interpreted so that it is equivalent to the logical expression ($\sim$p or q); symbolically, $p \longrightarrow q \equiv \sim$p or q. Thus, *modus ponens* can be written $[(\sim p \text{ or } q) \text{ and } p] \longrightarrow q$.

We are now in a position to observe what happens if both p and $\sim$p are true at the same time. No matter what the truth status of the proposition q (that is, for any arbitrary proposition q) ($\sim$p or q) will always be true since by hypothesis $\sim$p is true and the expression ($\sim$p or q) as a whole is true if only one of its components is true. By hypothesis, p is also true. Therefore, ($\sim$p or q) and p are both true, and the whole expression $\{[\sim p \text{ or } q) \text{ and } p] \longrightarrow q\}$ is true for any and all statements q no matter how absurd or inconsistent with known facts or principles they may be. However, if we admit absolutely inconsistent propositions into our storehouse of knowledge, then *modus ponens* we can derive the truth of any arbitrary proposition whatsover—which is absurd.

Logicians have gone to some lengths to preserve the fundamental status of the Law of Contradiction. For example, Quine (1960) appeals to the notion of "standards of translation" between one language and another to preserve the law from being violated. His argument is that if a translation from one language to another appears to violate the Law of Contradiction, then it is the translation that must be at fault. "Let us suppose . . . natives accept as true certain sentences of the form 'p and not p.' Or . . . that they accept as true a certain heathen sentence of the form 'q ka bu q,' the English translation of which has the form 'p and not p.' But now just how good a translation is this, and what may the lexicographer's method have been? If any evidence can count against a lexicographer's adoption of 'and' and 'not' as translation of 'ka' and 'bu,' certainly natives' acceptance of 'q ka bu q' count, overwhelmingly . . . prelogicality is a myth invented by bad translators" (Quine, 1960, p. 387). Quine further argues: "We impute our orthodox, [that is, classical] logic to the [deviant logician], or impose it upon him, by translating his deviant dialect" (1970, p. 81). Haack (1974, p. 15) notes in discussing the issue of rival logics to classical logic: "It is worth observing at the outset that this argument of Quine's . . . is incompatible with another thesis, . . . to the effect that none of our beliefs, the laws of logic included, is immune from revision in the light of experience. According to this view it is at least theoretically possible that we should revise our logic. . . . In principle at least, the possibility of revising logic is left open. However, the *Philosophy of Logic* thesis is that there can be no such thing as a real, but only an apparent, change of logic."

As the preceding comments suggest, the basic issue is the status of logic (or of formal methods of reasoning) within the scope of the sciences. It is beyond the scope of this book to review all the approaches that have been used to argue for the privileged status of logic. We shall merely mention two: an absolutist conception and a presuppositionist view.

According to the absolutist view, logical laws are unalterable "because they have a special status which guarantees their certainty" (Haack, 1974 p. 26). Kant was a proponent of this view: "There are but few sciences that can come into a permanent state, which admits of no further alteration. To these belong Logic and Metaphysics" (in Haack, 1974, p. 10). Although few logicians would now agree with Kant regarding the perfection, completeness, and unalterability of Aristolelian logic, the case can still be made that more modern versions of classical or two-truth logic are beyond revision. However, classical logic is itself but one theory of logic, and as such is not only subject to revision but to challenge by rival conceptions of logic.

The presupposition argument is that every science, in its basic desire to reason consistently, presupposes the existence and operation of logic. In this sense, logic is the most basic of the sciences since every science must have recourse to it. By itself this argument does not establish the privileged status of classical logic. To do this, one would have to show both that every science does indeed presuppose the existence of logic, and classical logic was uniquely presupposed. For another, the argument does not establish the unique fundamentalness of logic, for as Churchman has argued, it can be shown that every science presupposes the others. As Churchman has put it, "There is no sound reason why [an] inquiring system should start with logic. To be sure, all inquiry uses logic, but then, as we have seen, all inquiry uses every branch of inquiry. Logic itself can be regarded as a derivation of social communication, i.e., as a branch of sociology" (Churchman, 1971, p. 198).

We have emphasized this discussion of logic because of its fundamental importance to the AS's style of reasoning. Consider, for example, the simple schema X, A $\longrightarrow$ Y. Suppose that for the variables X, A, and Y, the general law $\{$X, A $\longrightarrow$ Y$\}$ has in fact been established so that X and A are both necessary and sufficient for the occurrence of Y. That is, suppose that the law "if X, A, then Y" has been established. Then the occurrence or presence of X and A is *modus ponens* sufficient to allow us to deduce the occurrence of Y: $\{$[(X and A) $\longrightarrow$ Y] and (X and A)$\}$ $\longrightarrow$ Y. In terms of this schema, we can understand once again the AS's preoccupation with precision, consistency, and logic. Given the precise measurement of X and A and the Law of Contradiction, we wish to be able to deduce with certainty the occurrence of Y. For a precise determination of X, A, we wish to be able to deduce the very particular Y which follows from X, A, and not any arbitrary consequence.

Philosophers of science, such as Hempel (1965, 1970), have invested considerable effort in the logical construction and interpretation of scientific theories. Indeed, if we take this line of reasoning far enough, in order to label something a scientific theory, we must be able to cast it into a logical form so that given the proper antecedent conditions (X, A), we can make a valid deduction (Y). This style of reasoning construes all scientific theories into this form, and unless something can be cast in this form, the AS tends to dismiss it as nonscientific.

Although we have examined a number of aspects of the AS's world view and have argued that they form part of an integrated whole, we have hardly exhausted the many dimensions of the AS's outlook or the many forms which the AS assumes in the social sciences. Instead, we have tried to capture the guiding spirit of the AS's scheme of reasoning.

FOUR

The Conceptual
Theorist

*There has always existed [a] set of antitheses or polarities, even
though, to be sure, one or the other was at a given time more
prominent—namely, between the Galilean (or, more properly,
Archimedean) attempt at precision and measurement . . . and, on
the other hand, the intuitions, glimpses, daydreams, and a priori
commitments that make up half the world of science in the form of
a personal, private, "subjective" activity.*

Gerald Holton (1973, 375)

Like the Analytic Scientist (AS) the Conceptual Theorist (CT) is
characterized by a broad and diverse set of attributes, some of
which are shown in Table 2. As with our presentation of the AS, we
shall begin with a discussion of the CT's general psychological
orientation. Nearly all the characteristics of the CT can be understood once it is appreciated that they derive from the CT's desire to
seek out or produce multiple explanations for any phenomenon.
Such multiple conceptual possibilities follow from their NT
(intuitive-thinking) orientation in the Jungian framework. Whereas
the AS works best within a single, well-defined, self-consistent
explanation or paradigm, the CT prefers to construct bridges between paradigms. Whereas the AS fundamentally believes that nature can be partitioned or broken down into divisible, precise fac-

tors, the CT believes that nature must be treated holistically and conceptually. Instead of there being a single, all-embracing, precise, internally self-consistent paradigm to treat all of nature's diverse phenomena, the CT believes that one must have recourse to many explicitly conflicting paradigms. In short, the CT believes that paradigms or models are only conceptual representations of reality, not reality per se, and that they serve primarily as stimulants to our conceptual imagination. Their purpose is to direct and to guide inquiry, not to constrain it.

The notion of conflict is central to the CT's world view. Whereas conflict or disagreement signals the breakdown of inquiry for the AS, the CT depends heavily upon the conflict or clash between different observers, theorists, and observations for intellectual stimulation. Whereas conflict signals the end of inquiry for the AS, it signals the beginning and sustaining point of inquiry for the CT.

Apparently, the CT is a speculative theorist who deeply values broad-ranging novel ideas, and who does not demand that these ideas be tied down to "reality" in the sense of being verified by accepted theories or facts. Indeed, the CT often prefers to challenge known facts and ideas, if only for the sake of speculative argument. Above all, the CT values the creation of novel conceptual possibilities, schemata, and hypotheses which allow us to revise, rethink, and challenge even the most firmly entrenched and accepted ideas. The CT believes that one must always be free to think and to invent the unthinkable in order to ferret out and challenge our most cherished, taken-for-granted ideas and assumptions.

Pierre Duhem and Paul Feyerabend are two well-known philosophers of science who espouse this view. In recent years, considerable attention has been focused in the philosophy of science on what is known as the Duhem or D-Thesis (Duhem, 1954; Quinn, 1969; Wedeking, 1969). Duhem (1954)—going against the nineteenth-century line of thought that while a scientific hypothesis could not be confirmed, it could be decisively falsified—argued that there can be no such thing as a completely decisive falsifying scientific experiment. Falsification followed a simple logical reasoning known as *modus tollens* (Churchman, 1940): if $H \longrightarrow O$ and if $\sim O$, therefore $\sim H$. That is, given a certain hypothesis H which implies a certain set of observational consequences O (if H is true,

Table 2. Characteristics of the Conceptual Theorist

	Evaluative categories	*Attributed characteristics*
External relations	Status of science as a special field of knowledge in relation to other fields	Occupies a privileged and preferred position, but is not clearly separable from other fields; no clear lines of demarcation; not autonomous or independent, no strict hierarchical ordering of fields; all depend upon one another; science is, however, value-free and apolitical.
Internal properties	A. Nature of scientific knowledge	Impersonal, value-free, disinterested, holistic, valid, apolitical, imaginative, multiple-causation, purposeful ambiguity, uncertainty, problematic
	B. Guarantors of scientific knowledge	Conflict between antithetical imaginative theories, comprehensive holistic theories, ever-expanding research programs
	C. Ultimate aims of science	To construct the broadest possible conceptual schemes; multiple production of conflicting schemas
	D. Preferred logic	Dialectical logics, indeterminate logics
	E. Preferred sociological norms (ideology)	Norms are a function of one's theoretical perspective and cannot be separated from one's conceptual-theoretical interests
	F. Preferred mode of inquiry	Conceptual inquiry; treatment of innovative concepts from multiple perspectives; invention of new schemas
	G. Properties of the scientist	Disinterested, unbiased, impersonal, imaginative, speculative, generalist, holistic

then we observe O), and also given that one has observed "not O" or ~O, then one can conclude *modus tollens* that not H or ~ H. In more compact terms, $\{[(H \longrightarrow O) \text{ and } \sim O] \longrightarrow \sim H\}$.

Duhem pointed that this schema is a gross oversimplification of the process of science. The scientist never tests a single hypothesis in isolation from other hypotheses but rather against a whole network of background assumptions, auxiliary hypotheses, broad metaphysical concepts, theories, and ideas. Therefore, Duhem concluded, a better representation of falsification was the more complicated schema

$$\left\langle \left\{ \left[\left(\sum_{i=1}^{n} H_i \right) \longrightarrow O \right] \text{ and } \sim O \right\} \blacktriangleright \sim \left(\sum_{i=1}^{n} H_i \right) \right\rangle.$$

Thus, when the observations of experiment (~O) were in disagreement with the predictions of theory (O), all that one was legitimately entitled to conclude was that one of the H_i making up the system of hypotheses, possibly infinite in number, was false; which particular hypothesis was in error (if indeed it was only one) could never be determined with complete assurance.

This is one of the major points of disagreement between the AS and CT. ASs believe that we can test hypotheses in isolation from one another and hence that over time we can distinguish false ideas from true ones with positive assurance and, in this sense at least, increase our knowledge of the world. For the CT the world is always more open ended and even ambiguous; indeed, this ambiguity is desirable, because it allows for flexibility, creativity, and free invention. The CT neither believes in, seeks, nor requires certainty in order to conduct inquiry.

Duhem did not contend that falsification never occurs and that experiments are therefore worthless but that the act of experimentation is inherently ambiguous—a risk-taking enterprise. Unless the scientist is willing to make some strong systemic assumptions, nothing of value is gained from an experiment. In order to test (falsify) a particular hypothesis, one has to assume (or discover by some means other than the current experiment itself) the veracity or plausibility of all the other hypotheses entering into the experiment. In this sense, science gives rise to policy disputes rather than settling them. For every question an experiment attempts to settle, it gives rise to more questions via the assumptions that were necessarily entertained in order to conduct the experiment. Since different scientists entertain different background assumptions, they might well reach very different conclusions.

In addition, Duhem argued that falsification was necessarily ambiguous in another sense. Suppose for the sake of argument we have a single isolated hypothesis entailing O and the results of some experiment which produces ~O. Even in this case a scientist is justified in concluding ~H *if and only if* he can show that there is no set of auxiliary assumptions that can "save the original hypothesis"; that is, that there exist no A such that $\{[H \text{ and } A] \rightarrow \sim O\}$—that H and A taken together are sufficient to deduce ~ O. Duhem did not assert that for *every* H it was possible to find a set of auxiliary assumptions or hypotheses A that would allow one to save H, but rather that "the burden of proof is on those who deny H to show that there does not exist an [A] which would make H compatible with ~O" (Laudan, 1965, p. 298). Unless it can be shown that there is no suitable A, a scientist is justified in continuing to believe in the power of the hypotheses even in the face of disconfirming or negative evidence.

The upshot is that one of science's most basic processes, that of hypothesis testing—the gradual elimination of false ideas through experiment—has a fundamental open-endedness to it. If experiments were irrefutably conclusive, and if observations themselves implied a single unambiguous interpretation, then the acceptance of scientific hypotheses would be as clear-cut as the AS wishes, and all scientists would be forced to the same set of background assumptions and a common interpretation of events. The implication is not that controlled experiments are worthless and thereby irrelevant to knowledge but rather that the compelling power of an experiment is dependent upon our ability to inspect its underlying background assumptions. As Churchman has put it: "There is no such thing as a "crucial test" in empirical science unless the [scientist] is willing to make some very strong presuppositions" (Churchman, 1971, p. 136). Thus, as much as we need a methodology for designing controlled experiments, we need even more a methodology for uncovering and analyzing the effect of underlying background assumptions.

Consider again the simple schema $\{[(H \longrightarrow O)$ and $\sim O] \longrightarrow \sim H\}$. Not only is this schema a gross simplification of scientific method for the reasons pointed out by Duhem, but it is seriously deficient on other grounds as well. Ever since Kant, it has been recognized that we cannot collect scientific data (Os) without having presupposed some prior theory with respect to what we are observing or wish to observe. In other words, observations are not theory free. While theories do not determine unequivocably what we will observe, they strongly influence what we can and do observe. Theories not only guide the design of experiments, but influence what we can extract from them. They serve, in short, as policy directives which make observation possible. Especially in science we do not merely open our eyes and observe free from prior theoretical expectations. "Seeing," as many philosophers have pointed out, is an activity of the mind, not solely of the eyes (Hanson, 1965, 1969, 1970). Observers from different theoretical perspectives do not in general "see" the same thing. Different theoretical perspectives strongly influence the interpretation we give to our observations.

The implications of this argument for *modus tollens* are considerable. Instead of the simple schema $\{[(H \longrightarrow O)$ and $\sim O] \longrightarrow \sim H\}$, we have instead the more complicated schema

$$\{[(H_i (T_j) \longrightarrow O (H_i, T_j)) \text{ and } \sim O (H_i, T_j)] \longrightarrow \sim H_i (T_j)\}.$$

That is, the hypotheses H formulated are a function of the theories T espoused; thus, $H_i = H_i (T_j)$. By the same token, $O = O (H_i, T_j)$, where O is a function of both H_i and T_j since the T strongly influence but do not solely determine the hypotheses H one formulates.

The provocative considerations of Paul Feyerabend (1975) enter at this point. Feyerabend argues that the testing of a scientific theory can be "incestuous": If theories and hypotheses strongly influence what we observe, then there is a real danger that observations, instead of challenging the theory and the hypotheses under scrutiny, will simply turn out to be most compatible with the theory and the hypotheses being tested. The theory and the hypotheses may unwittingly screen out the most critical or negative test observations, $\sim O$.

Feyerabend proposes a radical solution: Since observations can only be made through the use of theories and hypotheses, upon which the observations are based, and if the observations may unintentionally reinforce rather than challenge the theories upon which they are based, Feyerabend argues that the scientist has no alternative but to develop strongly competing alternate theories for every phenomenon. That is, if a theory can be construed as the conjunction of a series of propositions, then we wish to invent or discover at least two theories such that if $T_a = \bigcap tqa$, $T_b = \bigcap trb$, then $T_a \cap T_b = \phi$, where $\cap$ stands for the intersection symbol in set theory; in other words, $T_a^2 \bigcap tqa$ expresses the fact that T_a^2 is the conjunction of propositions tqa. We not only want the theories to have as little in common as possible $(T_a \cap T_b = \phi)$; we would also like each to be the dialectical opposite of the other $(tga \bigcap tgb = \phi)$ so that *modus tollens* the test observations $\sim O_b$ uncovered by one theory T_b will provide the strongest possible challenge to the predictions of the other theory O_a.

Combining the arguments of Duhem and Feyerabend results in a considerably more complicated schema for falsification. Instead of the simple version $\{[(H \longrightarrow O) \text{ and } \sim O] \longrightarrow \sim H\}$, we have

$$\langle\{[(\textstyle\sum H_i (T_j)) \longrightarrow O (\textstyle\sum H_i, T_j)] \text{ and}$$
$$\sim O (\textstyle\sum H_i, T_j) \longrightarrow \sim (\textstyle\sum H_i (T_j))\rangle$$

if and only if no $A (\sum H_i, T_j)$ can be found which "saves" $\sum H_i (T_j)$.

From this point of view, scientific method is considerably more open ended, complicated, and even precarious than envisioned by the AS. The scientist is not only required to make strong assumptions and value judgments within a particular theory but is also required to make strong assumptions and judgments between radically different theories in order to develop and test both of them, often simultaneously. No matter how well confirmed and established a previous theory is, the scientist is enjoined to invent the boldest, the most radical, and most speculative alternatives to the current established theory in order to mount the most critical test.

It is apparent that the psychological qualities demanded by this version of science are very different from those demanded by the AS's conception. Where the AS's conception demands the ability to work well within the confines of a particular, existing, precise, well-developed framework, the CT's conception demands the ability to work between several, often contradictory frameworks. Where the AS emphasizes precision, control, and the elimination of uncertainty, the CT emphasizes the increase of uncertainty by perpetually expanding and challenging accepted ways of looking at things. Whereas the AS devalues speculations and boldness in favor of methodological and methodical rigor, the CT stresses conceptual vigor.

Neither point of view—that of the AS or CT—is necessarily right or wrong, they are merely different. Even more important, each is more appropriate for a different stage of scientific inquiry. As we shall argue later, the CT's point of view is more appropriate for problem definition, hypothesis discovery and formulation, and conceptual theory building, but the AS's is more appropriate for systematic theory testing and theory building. AS science without CT science is narrow, parochical, and confining, reducing a potentially creative activity to a set of fixed rules and rituals—ultimately dogmatic scientism of the worst form. CT science without AS science can become merely fanciful speculation.

Although the CT's view of science may at first appear to violate the traditional concept of scientific inquiry, an increasing body of historical evidence supports this relatively imprecise style of inquiry. Westfall's (1973) provocative article in *Science,* "Newton and the Fudge Factor," is a good example. Westfall presents an impressive amount of evidence that Newton, over the course of his scientific career, repeatedly "brazenly manipulated" the evidence available at the time to fit in with his ideas—rather than the other way around. For example, with the data then available, Newton could not derive the inverse square law of gravitation. But because of his theoretical and aesthetic preference, the data were blatantly manipulated to fit in with the inverse square law. Newton's scientific editor, Roger Coates, called Newton's bluff. What ensued resembled a game of "musical numbers" in which Newton stretched the data first in one place and then in another. Westfall concludes by pointing out that while the *Principia* is testimony to Newton's genius as a scientist and mathematician, it is also testimony to the fact that "nobody can manipulate data like the master mathematician" (1973, p. 756).

This example is not intended to condone manipulation but to challenge our views regarding the procedures of science. If we draw the net of science too tightly, as the AS would prefer, then we leave out the bold, speculative, creative science of the CT. However, if we spread the net too broadly, we may let in cranks and crackpots. Cases such as Newton's provide the extreme challenge. Is Newton's manipulation of data allowable because he was ultimately proved correct, or was he proved correct—did his ideas gather widespread currency—because he was willing to risk a bold gamble and manipulate the data? Can we determine a priori the fruitful and legitimate manipulations from the unfruitful and illegimate? Do "great" scientists somehow have a warrant that lesser scientists do not have? Are great scientists great because their speculations have somehow proved fruitful or because they were willing to risk bold speculations in the face of extreme criticism from their peers?

Preferred Style of Inquiry

A recent article by Murray Davis, "That's Interesting! Towards a Phenomenology of Sociology and a Sociology of Phenomenology" (1971), represents a significant step toward the codification of the CT's approach. Davis's first thesis is that the great social scientists are not great because they produced "true" theories. Because theories are simplifications, they all become false at some point. While we usually think of some theories being more or less false than others, Davis contends that all theories fall into the class of "false" entities in the sense that the acceptance or utility of a theory—at least in the social sciences—is determined primarily on grounds other than truth per se. One of the main grounds for acceptance, Davis contends, is the "interestingness" of a theory. "A theorist is considered great, not because his theories are true, but because they are *interesting*. Those who carefully and exhaustively verify trivial theories are soon forgotten, whereas those who cursorily and expediently verify interesting theories are long remembered. In fact, the truth of a theory has very little to do with its impact, for a theory can continue to be found interesting even though its truth is disputed—even refuted!" (1971, p. 309).*

What is it that makes a theory or a theorist interesting? It is Davis's contention that an interesting theory is one which (1) identifies previously taken-for-granted underlying assumptions of a particular social science, (2) exposes, perhaps for the first time, the assumptions for critical and public scrutiny, (3) argues that a set of counter assumptions is actually more plausible. As Davis (1971, p. 313) puts it: "An *interesting* proposition [is] one which first [articulates] a phenomenological presumption about the way a particular part of the world [looks], and then [denies] this phenomenological presumption in the name of "truth," that is, in the name of a more profound, more real, more ontological criterion. Put more precisely, an *interesting* proposition [is] one which [attempts] first to expose the ontological claim of its accredited counterpart as merely phenomenological pretense with its own claim to ontological priority. In brief, an *interesting* proposition [is] always the negation of an accepted one. All of the propositions I examined were easily translatable into the form: 'What seems to be X is in reality accepted as X is actually non-X.'"

The uncovering and denial of assumptions is a complex social-psychological process. If a counterassumption merely affirms some aspect of an audience's set of background beliefs, the audience is likely to find the counterassumption obvious and uninteresting. Likewise, a proposition or counterassumption will be considered irrelevant and uninteresting if it does not speak to any aspect whatsoever of the audience's background belief. Finally, if a counterassumption denies the whole set of background beliefs, it is

*A classic case is Kuhn's (1962) theory of science. Kuhn's critics (Lakatos and Musgrave, 1970) have pointed out that nearly every one of Kuhn's contentions is wrong; for example, that there are almost no, if any, clear-cut examples of scientific revolutions as he defines them, that the term paradigm is fraught with innumerable difficulties. Yet Kuhn continues to be cited at an ever-increasing rate. The reason is that Kuhn has produced a fascinating theory of science in the sense in which Davis defines it. As a result, Kuhn's ideas will continue to live long after his critics' ideas have passed into oblivion. Kuhn's critics thereby miss one of the vital points of his book.

likely to be labeled absurd—and still uninteresting. To repeat: deny too little and be called trivial; deny too much and be called a crackpot. The history of science is replete with such cases, and although such rejection-can be partially explained as a sociological phenomenon, we suggest that it can also be partially explained psychologically—when CT ideas are narrowly judged from a strict AS perspective.

The following examples list the categories whereby one can judge, according to Davis, the "interestingness" of a proposition. The reader is directed to Davis's paper (1971) for liberal examples of the categories from the fields of psychology and sociology.

Single phenomenon

1. Organization

   a. What seems to be a disorganized (unstructured) phenomenon is in reality an organized (structured) phenomenon.

   b. What seems to be an organized (structured) phenomenon is in reality a disorganized (unstructured) phenomenon.

2. Composition

   a. What seem to be assorted heterogeneous phenomena are in reality composed of a single element.

   b. What seems to be a single phenomenon is in reality composed of assorted heterogeneous elements.

3. Abstraction

   a. What seems to be an individual phenomenon is in reality a holistic phenomenon.

   b. What seems to be a holistic phenomenon is in reality an individual phenomenon.

4. Generalization

   a. What seems to be a local phenomenon is in reality a general phenomenon.

   b. What seems to be a general phenomenon is in reality a local phenomenon.

5. Stabilization

   a. What seems to be a stable and unchanging phenomenon is in reality an unstable and changing phenomenon.

   b. What seems to be an unstable and changing phenomenon is in reality a stable and unchanging phenomenon.

6. Function

   a. What seems to be a phenomenon that functions ineffectively as a means for the attainment of an end is in reality a phenomenon that functions effectively.

   b. What seems to be a phenomenon that functions effectively as a means for the attainment of an end is in reality a phenomenon that functions ineffectively.

7. Evaluation

   a. What seems to be a bad phenomenon is in reality a good phenomenon.

   b. What seems to be a good phenomenon is in reality a bad phenomenon.

Multiple phenomena

8. Correlation

   a. What seem to be unrelated (independent) phenomena are in reality correlated (interdependent) phenomena.

   b. What seem to be related (interdependent) phenomena are in reality uncorrelated (independent) phenomena.

9. Coexistence   a. What seem to be phenomena which can exist together are in reality phenomena which cannot exist together.

                                    b. What seem to be phenomena which cannot exist together are in reality phenomena which can exist together.

10. Covariation   a. What seems to be positive covariation between phenomena is in reality a negative covariation between phenomena.

                                    b. What seems to be a negative covariation between phenomena is in reality a positive covariation between phenomena.

11. Similarity   a. What seem to be similar (nearly identical) phenomena are in reality opposite phenomena.

                                    b. What seem to be opposite phenomena are in reality similar (nearly identical) phenomena.

12. Causation   a. What seems to be the independent phenomenon (variable) in a causal relation is in reality the dependent phenomenon (variable).

                                    b. What seems to be the dependent phenomenon (variable) in a causal relation is in reality the independent phenomenon (variable).

Readers familiar with Kant's categories for synthetic judgments (1956) will recognize some striking similarities to Davis's categories. However, Davis's categories serve a different purpose. Whereas Kant's categories were deemed necessary for the perception of physical reality—what was necessary for the mind to presuppose or contain a priori to enable the act of perception—Davis's categories itemize the choices open to the designer of a social inquiry.

When Davis's principles are seen directly next to one another (1a and 1b, 2a and 2b), we can see the dialectical nature of the task facing the social scientist. In structuring an inquiry, not only does the social scientist have to choose which principle governs his inquiry (principle 1 versus 7, for example), but also which subprinciple applies (1a versus 1b).

Consider, for example, principle 12 (causation) and the difference between the AS's and the CT's approach to the choice between 12a and 12b. Let us say that 12a can be expressed as $X \longrightarrow Y$ and 12b as $Y \longrightarrow X$. The AS will reduce the problem to the "best" choice between 12a and 12b based on the degree to which 12a or 12b best fits in with the body of contemporary thought, ideas, and available data or facts and can most readily be expressed in a form such as the Campbell-Stanley (1969) framework outlined in Chapter Three. The AS, in other words, will reduce the problem to a single choice between 12a and 12b. In accordance with the AS's system of logic, 12a and 12b cannot both be true and both false.

The CT, in contrast, operates on a different intellectual wavelength. The CT will (1) identify which of the two, 12a or 12b, most accords with accepted thinking, theories, data, and facts; (2) try to determine whether a good, (or better) case can be made for the opposite or least accepted schema. In fact, the highest form of CT thinking will be constructing a dialectic between 12a and 12b. That is, what are all the reasons supporting 12a as a good representation of the two phenomena under discussion, and what are all the reasons supporting 12b as a good representation of the two phenomena under discussion (Churchman, 1971). Only if the social scientist has mounted the best possible case for these two antithetical representations of the same phenomena and one representation keeps coming up positive are we justified in accepting one schema over the other as a better representation of nature. In the extreme, we are enjoined to keep looking for a new way of expressing the opposition in order to keep the dialectic alive. The CT is directed not toward the quest for and resolution of conflict but toward the toleration, proliferation, and enjoyment of ambiguity and of multiple ways of viewing the world.

It is no accident that we have referred to this outlook as "conceptual exploration." Whereas the AS attempts to find the single schema that best represents the world, the CT is interested in exploring, creating, and inventing multiple possible and hypothetical representations of the world—even hypothetical worlds themselves. Further, the CT's emphasis is on the large-scale differences between these different representations rather than the details of any single schema. A potential danger of the AS is getting bogged down in infinite details; a potential danger of the CT is ignoring them altogether for the sake of comprehensiveness. ASs tend to suffer from "hardening of the categories"; CTs tend to suffer "loosening of the wholes."

The differences between the approaches of the AS and CT can be illustrated in terms of the notion of a means-ends schema. The AS is interested in the construction or discovery of a single means-ends such that max $V(S)$ can be attained where $V(S) = \sum_i \sum_j P(A_i)\, E_{ij} V_j$. V is defined as the relative expected value of a set of alternatives A_i of efficiency E_{ij} for obtaining objectives O_j of value V_j. $P(A_i)$ refers to the probability with which a scientist chooses a particular alternative to obtain O_j. E_{ij} is defined as $P(O_j/A_i)$. Further, the AS is also interested in discovering that particular course of action, call it A_k, such that the efficiency E_{kp} associated with A_k is maximal for the attainment of some preferred objective O_p of value V_p. Another way to put this is to say that the AS wishes to choose that particular A_k so that the usual type I and type II errors of statistics associated with the choice of A_k are minimized. That is, we want the probability of choosing some other course of action A_u when A_k is "true" to be minimal, that is, $P(A_u/A_k) = $ minimum; conversely, we also want $P(A_k/A_u) = $ maximum.

The CT, in contrast, is interested in the minimization of an entirely different kind of error called type III or E_{III}. E_{III} can be defined as the probability of attempting to solve the "wrong" problem or hypothesis instead of the "right" or "correct" problem or hypothesis. By "right," "wrong," and "correct," the CT means "more theoretically interesting" or "conceptually rich." Before the CT would attempt to minimize the type I and type II errors within a particular means-ends schema, he would first want to determine the correct schema (in the sense of theoretical fruitfulness or interest) to work on in the first place. What good, the CT asks, is it to solve the wrong problem precisely? As the statistician, John Tukey, once put it, "Far better an approximate solution to the right problem than an exact solution to the wrong one."

The CT's view is that the determination of the right versus the wrong schema can only be made comparatively, by comparing one means-end schema against another, whereas the AS formulates the problem of scientific explanation as selecting the single best course within a single means-end schema. The AS thus takes a micro-approach to the problem; the CT takes a macro-approach. Thus, the AS is engaged in testing the single-schema null hypothesis H_0 versus H_1, where

$$H_0: E_{kp} = E_{up}$$
$$H_1: E_{kp} \neq E_{up}.$$

The CT is engaged in testing the multiple schema null hypothesis H_0^1 and H_1^1 where

$$H_0^1: V(S_1) = V(S_2)$$
$$H_1^1: V(S_1) \neq V(S_2).$$

$V(S_1) = \sum_i \sum_j P(A_i) E_{ij} V_j$ and $V(S_2) = \sum_k \sum_m P(A_k) E_{km} V_m$ and $V(S_1)$ and $V(S_2)$ are the relative expected values of two different means-ends schemas.

In terms of H_0 and H_1, the type I error (E_I) can be defined as p (rejecting H_0/H_0 is true) and the type II error (E_{II}) can be defined as p (rejecting H_1/H_1 is true). In terms of H_0^1 and H_1^1, two different forms of the type III error (E_{III}) can be defined as follows:

$$E_{III}^1 = p \text{ (rejecting } H_0^1/H_0^1 \text{ is true)}$$
$$E_{III}^2 = p \text{ (rejecting } H_1^1/H_1^1 \text{ is true)}.$$

That is, we commit an E_{III} in the first case if we say $V(S_1) \neq V(S_2)$ when indeed $V(S_1) = V(S_2)$, whereas we commit an E_{III}^2 if we say that $V(S_1) = V(S_2)$ when $V(S_1) \neq V(S_2)$.

Notice that the foregoing relates to Davis's ideas on interestingness. If a substantial body of theorists believe that $V(S_1) = V(S_2)$, then the CT will attempt to show that a case can be made for $V(S_1) \neq V(S_2)$—to reject the null hypothesis. However, if it is believed that $V(S_1) \neq V(S_2)$, the CT will attempt to show that $V(S_1) = V(S_2)$ is worth considering—that there is no difference between two supposedly different formulations of an issue or problem.

Mitroff and Featheringham (1976) show how the choice between $H_0{}^1$ and $H_1{}^1$ can be put on an operational basis. Essentially the procedure involves the computation of $P[V(S_1) - V(S_2)]$: we test whether the difference between $V(S_1)$ and $V(S_2)$ is significant enough in statistical terms to warrant either rejection or acceptance of $H_0{}^1$. While this procedure may merely seem to repeat the method of the AS on a more global plane, it must be pointed out that while the computation of $p[V(S_1) - V(S_2)]$ involves knowledge of the detailed parts of the two means-ends schemas S_1 and S_2, S_1 and S_2 are only defined in enough detail to permit computation of $p[V(S_1) - V(S_2)]$. Indeed, the CT will not hesitate to speculate on different values of S_1 and S_2 in order to entertain the different theoretical possibilities for $p[V(S_1) - V(S_2)]$. The purpose of computing $p[V(S_1) - V(S_2)]$ for the CT is not so much to determine with exact precision "what is" as it would be for the AS, but rather "what if"—what would be signified if such and such were the case? This allows the CT to engage in his preferred inquiry pattern—conceptual, speculative investigation.

It should be clear by now that Campbell and Stanley's (1969) meta-criteria for the conduct of a theoretical investigation are very different from A. S. Davis's twelve criteria for the guidance and evaluation of a speculative investigation. Whereas the AS seeks to minimize E_I and E_{II}, the CT seeks to control E_{III} for the difference between different ways of conceptualizing the social world.

Preferred Sociological Norms (Ideology)

The trick in formulating those norms which are most distinctive of the CT's view is to keep firmly in mind the basic aim from which they result. The CT identifies the fundamental aim of science as the perpetual formulation of multiple, dialectical, interesting, global theories.

Given the CT's emphasis on the interestingness of a theory and the fact that what is interesting for one social group may not be for another, it should come as no surprise that the CT has a different interpretation of universalism from the AS. Universalism means that the acceptance or rejection of a proposition into the body of scientific knowledge is not supposed to depend on the personal or social attributes of the scientist advancing the proposition but only on the intellectual merits of the proposition itself (Merton, 1968, p. 607). The CT is in agreement with this principle only to the extent that the acceptance or rejection of a proposition should not depend on such irrelevant personal criteria as a scientist's race, religion, or social class. The CT insists, however, that the acceptance or rejection of a theory is a strong function of the assumptions that a particular scientific social group is willing and able to entertain. In this sense, the CT adheres to a norm of particularism: "The acceptance or rejection of claims entering the list of science is to a large extent a function of who makes the claim. The social and psychological characteristics of the scientist are important factors influencing how his work will be judged. The work of certain scientists will be given priority over that of others" (Mitroff, 1974a p. 59).

Particularism contends not only that different scientists and scientific groups do hold different assumptions but that they ought to. If all groups held to the same assumptions, then the challenging of assumptions by alternatives would be impossible. Since we never can be assured that we have arrived at the final correct set of assumptions, the CT argues that an absolutely necessary norm of science is the perpetual challenging of one set of assumptions by another. In this sense, science possesses a personal dimension (Polanyi, 1964).

Mitroff (1974a, 1974b) has argued that the need for challenging one's assumptions leads to the dialectical interplay between sets of contesting norms—norms and counternorms. It can be shown that the the CT's insistence on assumption challenging gives rise to a complicated dialectical normative structure of science. This structure is expressed in interplay between such opposing norms as emotional neutrality on the one hand and emotional commitment on the other; between organized skepticism on the one side and organized dogmatism on the other. Under the CT's world view, emotional disinterestedness is no longer a precondition for scientific inquiry as it is for the AS. Scientists need not be either individually or collectively unbiased; the CT accepts that scientists will be pre-disposed towards favorite theoretical assumptions. Indeed, it is only because scientists are committed to different assumptions that they are able to investigate the assumptions of their opposite numbers.

Preferred Logic

The concept of dialectical logic plays a central role in the CT's outlook and, as we shall see, in the dialectic among the four views of science which form the basis of this book. A number of systems have been proposed within the past ten to fifteen years for handling dialectic logic. For an eminently readable survey of these systems, the reader is directed to Wolf (1975). We wish only to note at this point that the presence of explicit contradictions no longer poses the serious threat to scientific explanation it once did. There exist formal systems of logic such that the expression (A and $\sim$ A) can hold for particular propositions; that is, these systems can handle explicit contradictions. This is generally done by defining the notion of implication so that, unlike classical logic, A$\rightarrow$B $\neq$ $\sim$ A or B. This means that the presence of A and $\sim$ A does not allow one to deduce the truth of any arbitrary consequence B (see Chapter 3). Unlike classical logic where if A and $\sim$ A are both true, the system as a whole suffers a "massive hemorrhage" or a "mass psychotic breakdown," the newer systems are able to handle contradictions without such total breakdowns. As Wolf has put it: "The central motivation behind construction [of these systems] is the insistence that just because a position is true, it is not necessarily implied by any other arbitrary proposition and just because a proposition is false, it does not necessarily imply all other propositions" (Wolf, 1975, p. 13).

There are also systems in which (A and $\sim$ A) is a local axiom—a property of the system itself for some of its propositions. Rather than merely being able to tolerate contradictions, these systems have an explicit built-in property (A and $\sim$ A). Generally these systems have to give up the concept of disjunctive syllogism, even its weakest form, in order to incorporate this property.

We are more concerned with the practical implications of dialectic logic for the practice of social science than we are with presenting the axiomitized structure of the newer formal dialectical logics. Such formal expositions are the subject of other treatises (see Wolf, 1975). For our purposes, a recent development in the concept of dialectics is important. This development leads to an actual procedure for conducting a dialectical debate (Mason, 1969). The procedure assumes that on any important social or scientific issue there are at least two different points of view. The procedure also assumes that underlying each viewpoint is a set of critical, largely implicit and unarticulated policy assumptions. The purpose of the procedure is to make these implicit assumptions explicit and line them up side by side with their counterassumptions from the opposing viewpoint. A debate is then conducted over the respective merit of the assumptions and counterassumptions (Mitroff and Emshoff, forthcoming). It is hoped that this procedure will lead to a better understanding of what each position entails and also provide a critical test of each side by forcing each side to face its most intense opposition.

Traditional discussions of dialectics have often missed this point. The simultaneous truth of A and ~A is not at stake.* The question is what is gained (or missed) by mounting the strongest possible arguments in favor of A side by side with the strongest

---

*As Kosok (1972) has cogently argued, neither A nor ~A is strictly true within either classical logic or dialectical logic. In a sense, all a dialectical logic does is to make explicit that both A and ~A are "fuzzy" in their ontology and epistemology; they are never fully formed or completely determined so that to speak of the strict truth or falsity of either A *or* ~A is simply not possible. A dialectical logic stresses the temporal interplay between A and ~A, that both are in the process of Becoming through their mutual and perpetual opposition to one another. A and ~ A are both true in the sense that to define the one is to define the other, even if only as a negative possibility. A and ~A are to be regarded as the end limits of an on-going dynamic process of interaction between knower and known, not as static, fully known objects of knowledge existing prior to the act of knowing itself. As parts of an on-going process, there is thus no contradiction in both A and ~A being "true" at the same time. (A and ~A) defines the boundary line between the not fully formed "objects" (A) and (~A). (For an excellent, intensive discussion, the reader is referred to Kosak, 1972.)

arguments in favor of ~A. We have just begun to develop dialectical decision theories or situations in which a decision maker is asked to review, judge, and act on the evidence in favor of and against a particular theory in the face of that theory's most severe opposition (Mason, 1969; Mitroff and Emshoff, 1977). As social scientists like Levine (1974) have argued, such theories of decision making may be a luxury in clear-cut cases, but they are a necessity in social science, where we deal with exceedingly complex situations and cannot presuppose universal agreement regarding assumptions.

The CT's argument is that a dialectical logic or process is appropriate to social science because conflict (1) is an important characteristic of social problems and issues, (2) cannot and should not be easily dismissed, and (3) is vital to the development of both methods and theories.

We have outlined the essence of the point of view identified with the Conceptual Theorist. Basic to the CT's position, we have argued, is a dialectical methodology for assessing the critical importance of the strategic assumptions underlying a theory. This position is more concerned with exposing and challenging assumptions than it is with building a single, self-consistent explanation of any phenomenon. Thus, it relishes and actively seeks out conflict and uncertainty because it does not regard contradiction or conflict as signifying the rational breakdown of inquiry but regards them as essential ingredients promoting the advance of inquiry. Unlike classical logic which regards A and ~A as fixed, already determined, and static categories, dialectical logic regards the presence of A and ~A as signifying that both A and ~A are in a dynamic state—that there is significant social debate regarding the status, meaning, and interpretation of A and ~A.

In a word, the conflict between A and ~A signals that there are at least two interpretations of the "same" event, and it is vital not to ignore this contradiction, for to do so would be to ignore an important social signal. Indeed, as we have argued, such signals supply the analyst with the opportunity to work backwards, as it were, to identify the different background assumptions they are making (Mason, 1969; Mitroff and Emshoff, 1977).

FIVE

The Conceptual Humanist

Humanity is alone real; the individual is an abstraction.

Auguste Comte

Conceptual Humanism (CH) is one of two methodologies based on feeling. They are the dialectical and psychological opposites of the thinking methodologies (AS and CT) presented in Chapters Three and Four. The Conceptual Humanist corresponds with the NF (intuitive-feeling) quadrant in the Jungian framework.

Table 3 lists the diverse characteristics of the CH. Rather than discussing the attributes in this table directly, however, we shall investigate these characteristics through the provocative ideas of the social psychologist John Rowan (1976a, 1976b), who has developed an interesting conceptual taxonomy of different patterns of inquiry that captures the spirit of the CH's approach to methodology.

Rowan envisions the research process as a cycle composed of five phases, each bearing a dialectical relationship to—that is, both affirming and denying—previous phases. In the affirmative role, each phase naturally follows from each previous phase and hence continues it. In the negative role, each phase contradicts, challenges, and attempts to change previous phases. The five phases

75

Table 3. Characteristics of the Conceptual Humanist

	Evaluative categories	*Attributed characteristics*
External relations	Status of science as a special field of knowledge in relation to other fields	Does not occupy a privileged and preferred position, is not clearly separable from other fields; no clear lines of demarcation; not autonomous and independent; all fields of knowledge depend upon one another. Science is not value-free; it is political.
Internal properties	A. Nature of scientific knowledge	Personal; value-constituted, interested activity; holistic; political; imaginative; multiple-causation; uncertain; problematic; concerned with humanity
	B. Guarantors of scientific knowledge	Human conflict between knowing agent (E) and subject known (S); inquiry fosters human growth and development
	C. Ultimate aims of science	To promote human development on the widest possible scale
	D. Preferred logic	Dialectical behavioral logics
	E. Preferred sociological norms (ideology)	Economic plenty, aesthetic beauty, human welfare
	F. Preferred mode of inquiry	Conceptual inquiry; treatment of innovative concepts; maximal cooperation between E and S so that both may better know themselves and one another
	G. Properties of the scientist	Interested; free to admit and know his biases; highly personal; imaginative, speculative, generalist; holistic

are: (1) Being, (2) Thinking, (3) Project, (4) Encounter, and (5) Communication. Rowan notes that different social theorists begin the research cycle at different phases and even lump some of them together in various ways. Because each phase feeds into the others and is dependent upon them, it makes little sense to talk of fixed starting or ending points. Indeed, these points on the cycle can be neither discussed nor distinguished from one another in complete isolation.

Rowan's preference is to start and end one cycle of the process with Being, loosely defined as "resting in one's own experience." More specifically, Being is the psychological sum of all these experiences (perceptions, sensations, feelings, thoughts) which lead to the personal recognition and affirmation of one's existence as a separate, autonomous human being. For Rowan, one starts the research cycle by "resting" in one's Being, that is, existing in one's set of currently accepted ways of doing things. "But at certain points the existing practices seem to be inadequate—one becomes dissatisfied. So the first [dialectical] negation arises; one turns *against* the old ways of doing things. A real problem has arisen" (Rowan, 1976a, p. 5).

We can see that the CH is very different from the CT. For the CH, a problem is defined by reference to the concept of one's personal being, whereas for the CT a problem, $P(t)$ is the discrepancy at time t between one's current capability of accomplishing some task or objective, $A(t)$, and what one would ideally like to be able to accomplish, $I(t)$—that is $P(t) = I(t) - A(t)$ (Mitroff, 1977).

The Thinking stage, while not exactly the same as Jung's concept of Thinking, bears some resemblance to it. Rowan's Thinking involves the formation of new theoretical possibilities, the attempt to construct new theoretical alternatives—what we have labeled conceptual-theoretical thinking (characteristic of the CT). This too leads to a stage of dissatisfaction, for at a certain point, the exploration of new theoretical possibilities must cease and one must move to the formulation of definite action plans. This is called the Project phase, and it involves risk taking and daring because it goes beyond the bounds of pure speculative or theoretical thinking alone.

The action phase itself is called Encounter. Like the other phases this is satisfying for a time. But ultimately it is not enough merely to act; one wants to reflect on the meanings of one's actions. This leads to Communication—sharing one's experiences with others so that they can learn from them.

Even communication must cease at a certain point unless one wants to become a permanent communicator. As Rowan puts it, one wants "to get back to some real work. Now that I know what to do, I can go happily into my field of work and continue there practicing [Being] what I have learned. Until . . ." (1976a, p. 5). And so the cycle continues.

The preceding broadly defined categories are reminiscent of the Conceptual Theorist. But where the CT musters his conceptual breadth to serve thinking, the CH musters it to serve feeling, which the CH interprets as serving people. The overriding concern of the CH is not how science, methodology, and experimentation can serve some abstract theoretical concepts of truth per se but how they further humanity as a whole.

The CH is interested in how science affects future generations. He is not content, like the AS, merely with the present. That for the CH is too short-sighted a view of human affairs. One must be concerned with the broadest and most far-ranging implications of one's methods if they are to be truly general and universal in scope. One's method must attempt to serve the largest collective good. The CH's motto is, "Better to fail in attempting to achieve the grand than to succeed in reaching the small."

The next step in the construction of Rowan's conceptual taxonomy of the research cycle consists in noting that at any phase (Being, Thinking, and so on), we can ask questions reflecting six concerns: (1) efficiency, (2) authenticity, (3) alienation, (4) politics, (5) patriarchy, and (6) dialectic. Efficiency questions have to do with the quality of various research designs (see the discussion of Campbell and Stanley, 1969, in Chapter Three) and with the formation of experimental hypotheses to test the selection of an appropriate research design, the choice of the appropriate statistical test, methods of data analysis, and so on. Much more interesting for our purposes is the concern of efficiency questions with the often-taken-for-granted divisions of tasks or roles within the experimental research setting. As we shall see, research conducted on the research setting itself has criticized the AS's concept of research because of the ill side-effects that result from the traditional role division between the research subject (S) and the experimenter (E).

Authenticity questions are concerned, on the negative side, with the alienation that often results from "hiding behind a role" such as the disinterested observer or the passive subject. On the positive side, authenticity questions concern the personal growth of the individuals involved in an experiment. This feature is vital to the CH. Indeed, the major criterion by which a CH judges an inquiry is: Will it lead to the personal betterment of the individuals involved in the inquiry and promise the greatest potential for bettering the largest number of individuals? An inquiry that increases knowledge at the expense of human welfare is very likely to be scorned by the CH. Indeed, truth at the expense of human welfare is likely to be questioned for its knowledge value. Why should a thing be regarded as "knowledge" if it does not lead to human betterment, even if only in the conceptual sense?

Alienation questions concern the trust, openness, growth, and self-determination promoted by an inquiry. That is, alienated research treats the subject as less than a human being, as an object to be manipulated by the E. Political questions ask whether the research unduly favors or hurts a particular social group, social structures, political regimes. Does it take for granted certain kinds of political oppression? Does it unwittingly portray one group in an unfavorable light? Patriarchal questions raise feminist concerns in particular. Does the research support or condone traditional male and female roles? Does it portray women (or men) in demeaning roles? Patriarchal questions raise the more fundamental issue of whether our traditional concepts of science itself are sexist.

Finally, dialectical questions concern whether one is oriented toward the production of a single, internally self-consistent version of a social experiment (as the AS is) or toward multiple and conflicting themes.

Table 4 shows the kinds of questions asked at each phase of the research cycle and illustrates the CH's departure from the AS's approach. At any phase we can ask efficiency, authenticity and other types of questions. The AS, placed within this context, would

Table 4. Questions Addressed To The Research Cycle

Type of Question	Being	Thinking	Phase of the Research Cycle		
			Project	Encounter	Communication
Efficiency	Is E familiar with the field, problem, literature; does she possess the requisite technical skills?	Can E break the problem down into specific researchable hypotheses?	Has the proper experimental design procedure been set up? Are questions operationally phrased?	Is the research being carried out in the intended way? Is E retaining her objectivity?	Are the results written up so that any outside observer could check them?
Authenticity	Is E aware of her own motives in doing this research? Does E work in a self-punishing way?	Does E believe she can be value free? Does she separate research from the rest of her life? Does she have something personal to gain from the research? Is she aware of this?	Is E investing herself fully and risking something personal?	Is E open to her feelings and able to express them in a genuine way?	Can E make the research results part of her own life?
Alienation	Can E listen to and involve others fully and care sincerely for them as people?	Does E deal with others strictly on a formal role basis?	Is the research plan psychologically fixed and rigid or open and flexible?	Is E open to S? Has trust between S and E been achieved? Is S running the show as much as E?	Can S make the results part of her own life?
Political	Is E aware of political forces supporting her?	Does E refuse to be politically isolated in her work?	What are the political implications of the research design?	Is the experiment such as to improve S's social situation?	Can other social groups benefit from the results?
Patriarchal	Is E sexist, racist?	Does E take patriarchy for granted?	Does the design take reinforced patterns of domination in any way?	Are control patterns confronted and broken down	Can society as a whole benefit?
Dialectical	Does E see the world in terms of conflicts? Does E see "the paradox of rhythm and the rhythm of paradox?" Does E see the necessity for paradox in every experiment?	Does E question positivistic findings? Is E looking for the major contradictions underlying her work?	Is the research planned to allow for the maximum of serendipity? Is E's own response built into the research plan?	Is conflict encouraged and being worked through? Is there an appreciation of ways in which quantity and quality interact?	Has the experiment made S and E more aware of their subjective interaction and bond?

Note: Rowan has used exclusively feminine pronouns in setting forth these questions; the nature of Patriarchal questions is well illustrated by this use of language.
Source: Adapted from Rowan, 1976a.

be restricted to asking efficiency questions in the design of an inquiry; in effect, all of Campbell and Stanley's (1969) meta-criteria are efficiency questions. As Rowan shows, however, there are a host of other concerns connected with the design of an inquiry. The Campbell and Stanley criteria only begin to tap the many concerns that must be confronted if one is to design a valid inquiry in the broadest sense of the meaning of "validity." For example, if S and E get to know and respect one another, is S more likely to give valid responses? Additionally, nowhere do Campbell and Stanley mention the moral aspects of an experiment. Is it legitimate to perform a certain experiment that adheres to strict efficiency criteria but is morally dubious? The CH demands serious consideration of such issues, whereas the AS might overlook or ignore them.

Table 4 presents only half of Rowan's story. The other half is illustrated by a series of diagrams which depicts the types of social science research traditions. In all, Rowan indicates thirteen different traditions, each illustrated by a circle with the different phases of the research cycle—Being, Thinking, Project, Encounter, Communication, back to Being—placed at points around a circle. The circle itself represents the movement of the researcher around the cycle. The subject of the experiment is shown as a line making contact with the circle. How and where the subject makes contact with the researcher (the circle) is what characterizes a particular research tradition or interaction pattern.

At any point in the research cycle, S and E can make contact through efficiency, authenticity, or any other issue illustrated in Table 4. Rowan prefers to concentrate most on alienation and authenticity, ostensibly because they represent his current interests. We believe that authenticity and alienation are two of the perennial concerns of the CH—in fact that they are the criteria which best differentiate the CH from "thinking" counterparts—the AS and CT.

For our purposes it will suffice to discuss five of Rowan's thirteen diagrams. They are shown in Figure 2. A dotted line or circle indicates that either S or E is "alienated"—that is without conscious relationship to each other. Thus a completely dotted circle indicates that E is out of touch with his feelings or alienated from himself, S, or both. The dashed lines indicate partial alienation; solid lines indicate nonalienation.

Figure 2: Five Types of Social Reseach

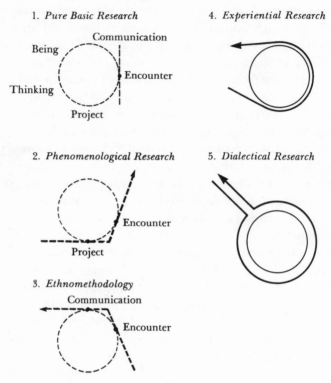

1. *Pure Basic Research*

Communication

Being

Encounter

Thinking

Project

4. *Experiential Research*

2. *Phenomenological Research*

Encounter

Project

5. *Dialectical Research*

3. *Ethnomethodology*

Communication

Encounter

Source: Adapted from Rowan (1976a).

The first diagram in Figure 2 represents pure basic research. The only contact between S and E is at the point of encounter—the point where S participates in an experimental setting, not of his own design (sometimes not even of his own choosing—for example, participation as part of a college course). As the dotted lines indicate, both S and E are alienated in this type of research. Their reactions to one another (and even to themselves) are controlled by a host of formal methodological procedures. Efficiency questions primarily are pursued around the circle; the other kinds of questions are either unnoticed, ignored, or suppressed.

The second diagram represents phenomenological research

(or ethnomethodology; see Heap and Roth, 1973). Rowan contends that in this kind of research the researcher is alienated from himself in the sense that he is being forced to adopt a very circumscribed philosophical perspective. The CH believes that the heavy intellectual and emotional investment made by this kind of researcher in certain abstract philosophical works—mainly the works of Heidegger, Husserl, Merleau-Ponty, and Schutz—actually alienate these researchers from themselves instead of liberating them. We agree with Rowan (1976a) that there is "more discussion of what the encounter is to mean than actual empirical research on it" in this tradition as a whole; for the most part, abstract discussions take place on what phenomenological research would look like if it were carried out. Thus, contact for E is made primarily at the Project stage with an S who may be alienated. However, since the purpose of this research is to discover S's world in his own terms, not in procedural terms dictated by the researcher, it is too much to say that E is completely alienated in the sense of being unable to appreciate the world of others.

Ethnomethodology (see Heap and Roth, 1973) is illustrated by diagram 3 of Figure 2. Rowan defines it succinctly as follows: "[The] researcher is alienated, but the subject may or may not be. Emphasis [is] on communication after an encounter, which may be nominal. The researcher is mainly interested in the unspoken assumptions which underlie social and psychological life, and the way in which these assumptions are covered up and hidden even from those who use them . . . a very inventive discipline" (1976a). Indeed, this inventiveness qualifies ethnomethodology as an intuitive methodology in the Jungian sense. What is not clear at this stage is whether ethnomethodology is more thinking or feeling in its orientation, and for this reason we agree with Rowan that it is only *partially* alienated. We view ethnomethodology as a thinking methodology; it merely has evolved an interesting strategy for uncovering social roles and the tremendous social energy which binds people to roles. To serve as a feeling methodology, it would have to be more concerned with involving Ss in the design of experiments and using the research generated to improve their self-awareness of taken-for-granted social roles.

Experiential and dialectical research, illustrated in diagrams 4 and 5, are most exemplary of the CH. Neither researcher nor subject is alienated in these forms of research; both strive to make full use of their thoughts, feelings, experiences, and intuitions to learn about themselves and one another. Perhaps the most distinguishing feature of these forms of research is the great stress laid on mutual exploration of the whole cycle by both researcher and subject. Indeed, E and S become cosubjects and coexperimenters as they jointly discover themselves, one another, and the issue to which they are attending. Alienation and authenticity questions are raised throughout, and great stress is put on the formulation and confirmation of hypotheses that attempt to produce a greater sense of awareness, growth, trust, and self-sufficiency in oneself and in others. Dialectical research in particular encourages explicit confrontation between the S and the E. A classic example of this kind of research is the studies of Jourard (1968), who was able to demonstrate that if he revealed some personal things about himself to Ss, then Ss were much more willing to reveal things about themselves on a questionnaire which called for the disclosure of highly personal information.

This completes our review of Rowan's excellent methodological taxonomy. We would like to point out that Rowan is not unique in these points. For another example of intelligent, perceptive criticism of traditional AS inquiry see Argyris (1973, 1974). Argyris, who reflects the CH position, uses an "assembly line" metaphor in his criticism of the traditional controlled experiment. Argyris argues that the conditions set up in most laboratory experiments are consonant with the repressive settings often found in prisons, schools, and mechanized assembly lines. The conditions are tight control, manipulation, and reward of desired behaviors as specified by the experimenter. Under such alienating circumstances, subjects often withdraw psychologically and physically from the experimental setting, exhibit overt hostility towards experimenters, exhibit covert hostility (such as deliberately giving wrong answers), emphasize being paid as reason for their participation, and even argue for safeguards (such as the formation of "unions of research subjects") to protect their interests.

Ultimately Argyris is critical of the controlled experiment not only on human grounds (it demeans both the subject and the experimenter) but also on methodological grounds (it fails to elicit valid generalizable information from subjects). The information gained from such settings may only be generalizable to other such settings, that is, repressive situations. The question then is: Given the deep entrenchment of AS thinking in our culture at large and in the social sciences in particular, what can be done to shift from an AS to a CH perspective? Are there any behavioral "technologies" available to produce a reorientation in values and outlook? And can these technologies be used to define more fully the CH's preferred mode of inquiry?

Preferred Style of Inquiry

The CH perspective as a scientific form is still emerging; thus, we must be speculative as we were in discussing the CT. Two recent research developments represent a significant advance toward a genuine CH methodology. Both developments arise out of research on small groups, particularly regarding interpersonal dynamics. The first development concerns the use of diverse groups to aid in one of the most widely neglected aspects of scientific inquiry—problem definition. The second development concerns the use of behavioral theory to affect changes in how people attempt to define and solve interpersonal problems. (This of course requires that people appreciate the first development—group problem solving—so the two developments are related.)

Problem definition is a vitally important phase of scientific inquiry—one that we feel has been sadly neglected. As McGuire (1973, p. 450) states:

> One drastic change that is called for in our teaching of research methodology is that we should emphasize the creative, hypothesis-formation stage . . . of research. It is my guess that at least 90% of the time in our current courses on methodology is devoted to presenting ways of testing hypotheses . . . Both the creation and testing of hypotheses are important parts of the scientific method, but the creative phase is the more important of the two. If our hypotheses are trivial, it is hardly worth amassing a great

methodological arsenal to test them: to paraphrase Maslow, what is not worth doing, is not worth doing well.

In terms of our concepts of E$_{III}$, we would add that it makes little sense to solve the "wrong" problem precisely (that is, in the AS mode).

Mitroff and Kilmann (1976) have utilized the Jungian framework (discussed in Chapter Two) to develop a methodology for problem definition. The first step is to bring together as diverse a group of individuals as possible who have an interest in the problem. The ideal group size is between 20 and 40 people. The second step is to administer an abbreviated version of the Myers-Briggs personality test (Myers-Briggs, 1962) in order to get a rough idea of the Jungian personality type of each individual (precise measurement of each individual is not necessary). The third step is to ask each person to write out his or her perspective of the problem at hand. (We have found that asking individuals to write out their view of the situation in the form of an idealized, open-ended story reveals the greatest differences between individual perspectives.) The fourth step is to put all individuals of the same personality type into a single group (all STs in one group, all NTs in another, and so on). Each subgroup is then asked to come up with a group view that reflects the consensus of the group. In this manner, four idealized perspectives of the problem or issue are produced. Generally the Jungian groups result in an intensification of the individual stories—the groups intensify the personality differences between the groups. For this reason, it matters less if we are off a bit in the personality measurement of any single individual. Also we have found that the groups experience little difficulty in reaching consensus because they are so similar.

The fifth step is to share the four perspectives with each group. In this manner each group not only has a chance to learn about themselves and how they view an issue but also how others who are different from them view it. The sixth step is to explain the Jungian typology to the participants so they can understand the underlying theoretical reasons for their differences. This step makes the whole procedure an example of a CH rather than a CT methodology. It is emphasized that no one type is right or better than the others; that the differences are important; that each perspective complements or supplements the others; and that each has its strengths as well as its weaknesses.

The seventh step is to push toward a synthesis of the individual perspectives of the issue into an integrated whole. This intuitive and holistic step is what makes this method conceptual rather than analytical. It demands that the individuals be prepared to rise above their individual perspectives. It would take us too far afield to describe how this is attempted. Synthesis is not merely a cognitive-intellectual affair, requiring a synthesizing idea sufficient to encompass the separate visions. It is also a profound socio-emotional affair, requiring that the participants appreciate the emotional stances of different social actors. To this end, we have found it necessary to employ value-clarification and organizational-development or team-building exercises to resolve the differences between the participants. These exercises are described in extensive detail elsewhere: the important point is the sharing of feelings, emotions, and human concerns which forms a vital and essential part of this methodology. For example, we often used the Thomas-Killmann conflict instrument (Thomas and Killmann, 1974) (1) to help individuals appreciate, tolerate, and handle the conflict between them and (2) to move toward integrative rather than distributive solutions to their problems. An integrative mode of problem solving emphasizes collaborative solutions—how opposing parties can both gain; in distributive solutions one only gains at the expense of the other. Integrative asks whether both parties can both get a whole or nearly whole pie by coming together. Distributive solutions are in effect "fixed pie" or zero-sum solutions.

The main difference between this method and the CT approach discussed in Chapter Four is that the purpose of this procedure is to help the individuals learn about themselves. The Jungian intuitive-feeling (NF) aspects of this procedure are apparent in the emotion of the situation. It is one thing to give an abstract, impersonal lecture on Jungian psychology and its potential applicability to problem definition. It is quite another for individuals to witness the human implications of the schema in terms of their own personal perspectives. To repeat—the purpose of the procedure is not only for the participants to see that what each group instinctively takes as a "natural" definition ("given") of the problem another takes in a very different manner (as an unwarranted "taken"), but for the participants to achieve self-understanding through a sharing of themselves through others.

This series of steps can be generalized to a research methodology consistent with the CH approach. The seven steps were specifically concerned with "testing" the Jungian typology to determine whether the framework does indeed account for differences among individuals and groups. However, the subjects themselves are actively involved in hypothesis formation, assessment, and the learning process—along with the experimenter—rather than serving as passive, uninvolved objects of experimentation. Using a similar approach, an experimenter could "test" other personality frameworks or measuring instruments, social science paradigms, and so on, by actively involving people, as individuals and groups, in the phenomenon being tested—discussing with the experimenter how they feel, how they think, and basically what they are experiencing. Finally, a community judgment can be made of the "validity"—that is, the usefulness and relevance to the subjects—of the phenomenon or concept in question.

Naturally, one could develop a systematic, standardized set of steps for such a process. But we must question whether at some point such standardization will transform the CH approach into the AS approach. What is most important to the CH is that the process for involving people in scientific inquiry is flexible and geared to foster meaningful data—for both experimenter and subjects—and that nonalienation is as important as standardized data.

Preferred Logic

Argyris and Schön, in their book, *Theory into Practice: Increasing Professional Effectiveness* (1974), attempt to construct a behavioral theory of dialectics. While the preferred logic of both the CH and the CT is dialectical, there is a vast difference in the brand of dialectics practiced and espoused by each. The dialectical logic of CT is formal and cognitive—it is a thinking-based logic. The dialectical logic of the CH, in contrast, is behavioral and interpersonal—it is a feeling-based logic. (By *logic* we mean a style of conceptualizing reality, not just the strict sense of formal logics.) The work of Argyris and Schön is dialectical because it is based on the explicit confrontation between persons and ideas at several distinct levels. The most basic level of confrontation is between what an individual says or thinks (espoused theory of action) and what he or she actually does (actual theory in use).

Argyris and Schön start with the fundamental assumption that all individuals operate with one of two basic behavioral models of the world: Model I, Theory-In-Use, and Model II, Ideal Espoused Theory. Each model is characterized by (1) governing variables, (2) preferred action strategies, (3) consequences for the behavioral world, (4) consequences for learning, and (5) behavioral effectiveness. The two models differ significantly in their underlying dimensions, and there is a tendency on the part of individuals to say that they act in accordance with Model II (their ideal espoused theory) when their actual theory-in-use accords with Model I. Thus there is a fundamental tension, not always apparent to the individuals themselves, between what they say they do (or ideally would like to do) and what they actually do.

The characteristics of Model I, as identified by Argyris and Schön with participants in their study (1974, pp. 66–67), are:

1. Define goals and try to achieve them: Participants rarely tried to develop a mutual definition of purposes with others, nor were they open to being influenced to alter their perception of the task.
2. Maximize winning and minimize losing: Participants felt that once they had decided on their goals, changing them would be a sign of weakness.
3. Minimize negative feelings: Participants were almost unanimous that generating negative feelings showed ineptness, incompetence, or lack of diplomacy. Permitting or helping others to express their negative feelings was seen as a poor strategy.
4. Be rational: Be objective and intellectual, suppress your feelings, and do not become emotional.

The effect of these characteristics, when translated into individual and organizational patterns of action, is a self-sealing system of behavior. The premises upon which the system are built are defensive and may exclude any data that challenge them. There is no breaking out of this vicious circle; lack of interpersonal communication tends to promote more of the same.

Model II (Argyris and Schön, 1974, pp. 86–89) is founded on a diametrically opposed set of governing variables:

1. Maximize valid information: This primary governing variable justifies the other variables. It implies that the actor provides others with observable data and reports so they can make valid attributions about the actor. It also means creating conditions that will lead others to provide observable data and reports that will enable the actor to make valid attributions about them.
2. Maximize free and informed choice: "A choice is informed if it is based on relevant information. The more an individual is aware of the values of the variables relevant to his decision, the more likely he is to make an informed choice. A choice is free to the degree to which the individual making it can: define his objectives; define how to achieve these objectives; define objectives that are within his capacities; and relate his objectives to central personal needs whose fulfillment does not involve defense mechanisms beyond his control" (1974, p. 88).
3. Maximize internal commitment to decisions made: The individual feels responsible for his own choices and is committed to an action because it is intrinsically satisfying—not, as in the case of Model I, because of reward or penalty for a certain action.

Argyris and Schön prefer Model II as a research methodology: "Traditional research tends to create subject-researcher relationships that are congruent with Model I. Rather than reinforce this type of professional technique, one goal is to develop methodologies and instruments that are congruent with a Model II world. If this could be accomplished, research activities and learning activities would reinforce each other; this, in turn, could offer feedback that increases the probability that subjects would try to give us minimally distorted information" (1974, pp. 93–94). (See Jourard, 1968, for an excellent example of the effect of Model II on experimental results.)

If research methods and instruments are to approximate Model II, four qualifications must be applied (Argyris and Schön, 1974, pp. 93–94): (1) The research design cannot be masterminded and unilaterally controlled by the researchers, nor can subjects be requested to cooperate simply in order to contribute to knowledge about human behavior. (2) The instruments used must produce directly observable data that can be used by subjects to implement their own learning experiences. (3) All hypotheses must be openly stated. The research relationship should be designed so that subjects have a personal interest in providing valid information; thus, public statement of variables and hypotheses would not cause them to distort the data. (4) Subjects must be so interested in the public and rigorous testing of hypotheses that they continuously monitor researchers' behavior.

It is beyond the scope of this book to describe in detail the techniques used by Argyris and Schön to help individuals shift from Model I to Model II behavior. One point, however, stands out to them and to us: The instructor (facilitator, interventionist) must not use Model I behavior in attempting to shift individuals from Model I to Model II. Instead the change from Model I to Model II must be accomplished with techniques consistent with Model II.

One effective tool in Argyris and Schön's system is the setting of behavioral dilemmas which force the recognition of the gap between individuals' ideally desired and espoused theory of behavior (Model II) and their actual theory-in-use (Model I). We call this technique the setting up of *personal dialectics*—an explicit tug-of-war between two personal views of the world. Dialectic here is not abstract or theoretical; rather, it implies confrontation at deep levels of existence between what one has pretended to be and what one thinks one would like to be. The instructor's role in this situation is therapeutic: to guide the novice, with as much understanding and love as possible, through a difficult transition—if not a crisis. The instructor must help the participants evaluate their old world view while at the same time setting up conditions that will allow them to have positive experiences of the new world view. Participants must retain the freedom to go back to Model I if they so desire. To force every human being to be compatible with Model II would destroy the dialectic.

Preferred Sociological Norms (Ideology)

The ideal aims that the CH attributes to science are: (1) the generation of "valid information" in the behavioral or human sense (information that affects the human condition); (2) the ability to make free informed choices; and (3) the ability to form commitment to one's choices. Thus, when researchers such as Argyris (1973, 1974) formulated the aims of the intervention process, they articulated a different set of aims for science from the traditional AS goals (see Chapter Three).

In the broadest sense, the overriding aim of science for the CH is the greatest increase in human welfare for the largest number of people. Under this view, science is anything but an autonomous institution, existing solely for its own sake, and governed by abstract methodological rules and aims. The ultimate test is the universal betterment of mankind. Ackoff and Emery (1972) have attempted a complete formulation of the CH's aims, including (1) economic plenty, (2) perfect self-knowledge and knowledge of one's environment, (3) peace of mind as reflected in the ideal ethico-moral state of the good, and (4) the aesthetic state of beauty. Given the dominance of AS aims or norms in our traditional concept of science, the strangeness of these items is no surprise. It has long been recognized that aesthetic considerations play a strong role within science. But whereas the CT (such as Davis) is fascinated with the interestingness of a theory, the CH is fascinated with the aesthetics of a theory, because one of the aims of science is the increase of beauty in the world. What good does it do one's soul to have the biggest and most theoretically sound science if it does not increase beauty in the world—or worse if it increases the ugliness of modern life?

According to C. West Churchman (1971, p. 178), "The Hegelian inquirer is a storyteller, and Hegel's Thesis is that the best inquiry is the inquiry that produces stories. The underlying life of a story is its drama, not its 'accuracy.' . . . But is storytelling science? Does a system designed to tell stories well also produce knowledge?" In summarizing the CH view of science, we repeat Churchman's question: "Is storytelling science?" For the CH the answer is "yes." This does not mean that any story qualifies as science but that science consists of taking stories seriously. Stories can be used in a variety of ways: as amusement or as devices with which to peer into human desires, wishes, hopes and fears. In this sense, stories form an essential ingredient of the CH's method because they provide the "hardest" body of evidence and the best method of problem definition.

The best stories are those which stir people's minds, hearts, and souls and by doing so give them new insights into themselves, their problems, and their human condition. The challenge is to develop a human science that more fully serves this aim.

The question then is not, "Is storytelling science?" but "Can science learn to tell good stories?"

SIX

The Particular
Humanist

*Loving is a way of knowing, and for loving to know, it must
personify. Personifying is thus a way of knowing, especially
knowing what is invisible, hidden in the heart.*

James Hillman (1975, p. 15)

Of all the world views described in this book, the Particular
Humanist (PH) represents the greatest challenge to our contemporary ideas regarding science. While Conceptual Theoreticism
and Conceptual Humanism somewhat challenge conventional
analytic science, Particular Humanism is an even greater challenge
(although the dividing line between CH and PH is exceedingly thin
at times).

Table 5 represents a few of the characteristics of the PH.
Nearly all these characteristics can be understood once it is appreciated that they derive from the PH's intense concern with capturing and describing the uniqueness of particular individual
human beings. The PH naturally treats every human being as
though he or she were unique—not to be compared with anyone or
anything else. Thus, the PH is not interested in formulating general theories of human behavior at all—not so much because this is
impossible (although the PH argues it *is* impossible) but because it is

Table 5. Characteristics of the Particular Humanist

	Evaluative categories	Attributed characteristics
External relations	Status of science as a special field of knowledge in relation to other fields	Does not occupy a privileged and special position; may be subordinate to poetry, literature, art, music, and mysticism as older, "superior" ways of knowing
Internal properties	A. Nature of scientific knowledge	Personal, value-constituted, interested; partisan activity; poetic, political, action-oriented; acausal, nonrational
	B. Guarantors of scientific knowledge	Intense personal knowledge and experience
	C. Ultimate aims of science	To help *this* person know himself or herself uniquely and to achieve his own self-determination
	D. Preferred logic	The "logic" of the unique and singular
	E. Preferred sociological norms (ideology)	Counternorms to CUDOS
	F. Preferred mode of inquiry	The case study; the in-depth, detailed study of a particular individual
	G. Properties of the scientist	Interested, "all-too-human," biased, poetic, committed to the postulates of an action-oriented science

not desirable. To study people in general, even from a humanistic perspective (like the CH's) is for the PH inevitably to lose sight of the unique humanity of an individual—to fail to capture precisely *this* person. The PH takes to heart Kant's dictum to treat everyone as a unique means rather than an abstract, theoretical end.

Ernst Cassirer (1955, p. 74) discusses science in relation to mythology. As we shall see, there is a close affinity between myths and the PH's concept of social reality: "Whereas scientific thought [AS] takes an attitude of inquiry and doubt toward the 'object' with its claim to objectivity and necessity, myth knows no such opposition. It 'has' the object only insofar as it is overpowered by it; it does not possess the object by progressively building it but is simply possessed by it. It has no will to understand the object by encompassing it logically and articulating it with a complex of causes and effects. . . . Instead of being bound by the schema of rule, a necessary law, each object that engages and fills the mythical consciousness pertains, as it were, only to itself; it is incomparable and unique. It lives in an individual atmosphere and can only be apprehended in its uniqueness, its immediate here and now." The rest of this passage shows how thin the dividing line is between CH and PH: "Yet on the other hand the contents of the mythical consciousness do not disperse into mere disconnected particulars; they, too, are governed by a universal principle—which, however, is of an entirely different kind and origin from the universal principle of the logical concept [of the CH]. . . . It is this characteristic *transcendence* which links the contents of the mythical and religious consciousness [of the PH]" (p. 74).

Preferred Style of Inquiry

There are two parts to the PH's preferred methodology. The first has to do with vehicles the PH uses to gather his material and the typical focal point of his material. The second has to do with the unique manner he has deliberately adopted for conveying the results of his material. Both aspects we would emphasize are strongly coupled together in the sense that they naturally build upon and complement one another.

The case study (see Diesing, 1971) is the method emphatically preferred by the PH because the case study focuses on the primary object of the PH's concern—the in-depth detailed rendering of the **life space** of a single individual or social group. (By life-space the study means capturing the total sense of an individual's world, not just a part of it as in the AS approach.) The AS condemns the case study; the CH uses it as one of several methods; the PH supports the case study as the most appropriate style of inquiry.

For the PH, all knowledge derives from a personal context, what Polanyi has labeled "personal knowledge" (1964). The act of knowing and its product, knowledge, cannot be severed from direct interaction between the knower and the thing to be known. No amount of quantitative sophistication or theoretical generalization can substitute for the physical presence of a concerned, caring, human observer and the interaction that takes place between observer and observed. Indeed, it is this interaction that guarantees for the PH the possibility of observing and the validity of what is observed. It is inconceivable to the PH that without in-depth human interaction one would get to know *this particular* man precisely as a man. The subtleties of the human spirit are such that they demand an intense human relationship in which they can be observed.

From the preceding it follows that a good part of the method of the PH is participant observation with the added dimension of "co-participant" interaction or involvement. A phrase that describes the PH's style of interaction is "mutual therapy." The PH's aim as a scientist is to interact with another human so that both the PH and the other person will be physically and psychologically improved by the relationship. Such improvement is impossible without a mutual, trusting relationship, and anything that does not further the development of this relationship is rejected by the PH.

The form in which the PH presents scientific results is very important. The preferred format is a personalized descriptive account of real human characters (see Hillman, 1975a, 1975b). Every attempt is made to capture the richness of detail of the lives of the characters: their strengths, weaknesses, hopes, dreams, and fears. One of the central characters in the PH's write-up is the researcher him- or herself—not because the PH has an unyielding ego but because of a fundamental belief that one cannot know the object of the researcher's interests without also knowing about the researcher. The objectivity of the PH's method is based on the visibility of all the subjective biases of the researcher. Thus the PH must be ruthless in exposing the motives for a particular study, and in fact nearly every study done in this tradition contains a preface or appendix wherein the researcher discusses publicly his or her motives and personal reasons for doing the study and feelings that emerged as the study was performed. From the PH's viewpoint, one's work and one's life cannot be separated; the two inform one another. Thus sharing one's feelings about one's work is inseparable from sharing feelings about one's life in general.

Torbert (1976, p. 168) describes with great clarity the state of mind of such a researcher: "So my thought explores various lines actively, interrupting tangents acceptingly, alert instead to radii— to movements of intuitive integration that move me simultaneously outwards towards my social errand of writing and inwards towards a spiritual centre. I seek to verbalize certain ideas in order to make them socially accessible and the same time to remain inwardly enlightened in order to continue to see the patterns I translate into ideas and words."

Torbert has proposed four "intuitive axioms" for the personal practice of an action-oriented science. An axiom for Torbert is not the impersonal, theoretical, formal statement of the AS but rather a representation of the complete personalization of every aspect of science. "Through this kind of research, intuition, feeling, action, and effect become simultaneously illuminated by one's attention and thereby can begin to struggle towards mutual congruence" (p. 167).

Torbert's first axiom (1976, pp. 167–168) holds that a person must undergo an unimaginable amount of self-development before becoming capable of valid action. This self-development includes simultaneous disciplining and freeing of emotions, behavior, and one's capacity for higher thought—thought capable of tracing the patterns of intuition, feelings, and behavior. Such thought is necessary if one is to engage in inquiry and realize possibilities while in action rather than simply reflecting on what might have been after the fact.

The second axiom holds that such higher thought-feeling patterns can not be accomplished without other people. For the PH, the scientist requires an intimate circle of friends who serve as a personal support group to help the individual realize his or her full human potential. "It appears that the genuine intimacy that would be the hallmark of such a circle of friends is, on the one [hand], not approached by most persons, who prefer to surround their close relationships with privacy, habit, and unexamined personal or cultural premises, and is, on the other hand, overleaped by historically great men of truth, who achieve their culture-transcending integrations in solitude" (1976, p. 172).

Based upon these reflections, Torbert offers his third and fourth axioms. The third axiom is that even the first steps on the path toward action science have unavoidable, immediate, and strong social consequences, even if the researcher is not ready to take social action and does not intend to change others. Since action science concerns one's own life in relation to others, "there is no safe cadaver to practice on, no setting from which one is emotionally disconnected to study. At best, one's early errors in observation and experiment may be protected from disastrous consequences by corrective feedback from trustworthy, unthreatened friends" (1976, p. 172). The fourth axiom of social science holds that "objective timing is of the essence to relationally valid action. This axiom directly contradicts the effort of reflective academic science [AS and CT] to develop a theory generalizable to all times and places. It also contradicts most persons' tendency to settle into, or try to justify, one particular style of social behavior as more effective than others" (1976, p. 173).

Preferred Logic

On the surface, the PH seems strongly opposed to the concept of a logic, with abstract, depersonalized categories. Actually, the PH is merely opposed to the AS's concept of logic. Indeed, from the previous viewpoints we have considered, the PH's logic is foreign and paradoxical. If the AS views the CH's concept of logic as hopelessly vague and befuddled by irrelevant behavioral concerns, then the PH's logic is, to the AS, downright bizarre and beyond comprehension. Although he strongly disagrees with it, the AS can at least understand what the CT is getting at. In the AS's scheme of things the CH is hopelessly misguided. The PH is simply "off the deep-end." In the strict sense, the PH's contribution to logic takes the form of a challenge: Is a formal logic of Feeling (in the Jungian sense) possible? Can the PH's style of reasoning be captured by formal methods, that is, represented within some abstract formal system?

The first difficulty in constructing such a formal logic has to do with the relationship of the parts of the PH's world to the whole. Another difficulty arises in making sense of the logical operators between elements.

Mythical thought, with its emphasis on personalization and storytelling, is analogous to the relationship between the parts and the wholes of the PH's world. In our everyday world and in ordinary science, the parts of an entity are strictly subordinate to the whole. This is not true in mythical thinking, where the part is more than just a part. By its very presence, the part signifies the whole and becomes, as it were, identical with it. Cassirer (1955, pp. 64–65), expands this point: "The whole is the part, in the sense that it enters into it with its whole mythical-substantial essence, that it is somehow sensuously and materially 'in' it. The whole man is contained in his hair, his nail cuttings, his clothes, his footprints. Every trace a man leaves passes as a real part of him, which can react on him as a whole and endanger him as a whole. . . . Mythical Thinking does not know that relation which we call a relation of logical subsumption, the relation of an individual to its species or genus, but always forms a material relation of action and thus—since in mythical thinking only 'like' can act on 'like'—a relation of material equivalence."

This first difficulty—distinguishing between parts and wholes, which the PH sees as identical—leads us to the second difficulty—how to operate or work on the elements of this logic. Actually, since the elements (parts) can at least be distinguished by referring them back to their whole, the first difficulty is not insurmountable. The second, however, has no current or foreseeable solution. Even worse, the authors know of no logicians who are currently working on the problem, let alone sensitive to it. If the very heart of a PH methodology is a rendering of unique particulars in extreme detail, how can one combine the unique particulars of, for example, a single researcher into a generalizable whole (not to mention the particulars of diverse researchers)? In short, if at the core of science is the concept of generalization, is a science (or logic) of the unique possible?

Cowan (1975, p. 594) expresses our concerns as follows:

> The situation calls for the development of a logic of the singular and a mathematics of the singular: Empirical mathematics, the mathematics not of induction from particular instances to general rules, but the mathematics of actually existing unique objects or events. . . .

> I haven't the faintest idea what a mathematics of singularity would be like. I only know what it would not be like. That is to say, it would not be generalized. So, too, for a logic of singularity. In such a logic, the principle of substitutability would not operate. Nor would transitivity. Identity itself would have only a special reference. . . . Every one of the operations would have to be redefined.

We cannot at this time predict whether the kind of logic discussed by Cowan will come into being. However, the failure of such a logic to materialize need not constitute a serious impediment to the scientific status of the PH methodology. The fact that the problems involved in a science or logic of the unique can be clearly stated is itself an important concession for traditional (AS) science. We prefer to think of the PH's challenge to traditional science as a newly emerging, distinctive form of inquiry rather than an altogether nonscientific phenomenon.

Preferred Sociological Norms (Ideology)

In our original conception of this book, we viewed the AS and CH styles and the CT and PH styles as dialectical pairs. But the more we reflect on the psychological forces underlying the styles of inquiry, the more we feel that the AS and PH are most dialectically opposed. It is not the opposition between AS (Sensing-Thinking) and PH (Sensing-Feeling) that is at issue but the basic opposition between Thinking and Feeling; the AS and PH styles best capture this fundamental divergence (Kilmann and Mitroff, 1977).

In an earlier work, Mitroff (1974a, p. 592) described the substantive nature of the opposition. The following list portrays the opposition in the form of opposing norms and counternorms. The items on the left refer to AS characteristics described in Chapter Three. Two additional norms have been added to this side to reflect the fact that the original set (first postulated by Merton, 1968) has been expanded by others. Barber (1952) for example has added "faith in the moral virtue of rationality" and "emotional neutrality." For every norm characteristic of the AS's view, a case can be made for a dialectically opposite counternorm characteristic of the PH view, and these counternorms express the personalization of science.

Norms	Counternorms

1. *Faith in the moral virtue of rationality* (Barber, 1952).

2. *Emotional neutrality* as an instrumental condition for the achievement of rationality (Barber, 1952).

3. *Universalism:* "The acceptance or rejection of claims entering the list of science is not to depend on the personal or social attributes of their protagonist; his race, nationality, religion, class and personal qualities are as such irrelevant. Objectivity precludes particularism. ... The imperative of universalism is rooted deep in the impersonal character of science" (Merton, 1949, p. 607).

4. *Communism:* "Property rights are reduced to the absolute minimum of credit for priority of discovery" (Barber, 1952, p. 130). "Secrecy is the 'antithesis' of this norm; full and open

1. *Faith in the moral virtue of rationality and nonrationality* (cf. Tart, 1972).

2. *Emotional commitment* as an instrumental condition for the achievement of rationality (cf. Merton, 1963a; Mitroff, 1974b).

3. *Particularism:* "The acceptance or rejection of claims entering the list of science is to a large extent a function of who makes the claim" (Boguslaw, 1968, p. 59). The social and psychological characteristics of the scientist are important factors influencing how his work will be judged. The work of certain scientists will be given priority over that of others (Mitroff, 1974b). The imperative of particularism is rooted deep in the personal character of science (Merton, 1963a; Polanyi, 1958).

4. *Solitariness* (or "Miserism" [Boguslaw, 1968, p. 59]): Property rights are expanded to include protective control over the disposition of one's discoveries; secrecy thus becomes a

communication [of scientific results] its enactment" (Merton, 1949, p. 611).

5. *Disinterestedness:* "Scientists are expected by their peers to achieve the self-interest they have in work–satisfaction and in prestige through serving the [scientific] community interest directly" (Barber, 1952, p. 132).

6. *Organized skepticism:* "The scientist is obliged ... to make public his criticisms of the work of others when he believes it to be in error ... no scientist's contribution to knowledge can be accepted without careful scrutiny, and that the scientist must doubt his own findings as well as those of others" (Storer, 1966, p. 79).

necessary moral act (Mitroff, 1974b).

5. *Interestedness:* Scientists are expected by their close colleagues to achieve the self-interest they have in work-satisfaction and in prestige through serving their special communities of interest, e.g., their invisible college (Boguslaw, 1968, p. 59; Mitroff, 1974b).

6. *Organized dogmatism:* "Each scientist should make certain that previous work by others on which he bases his work is sufficiently identified so that others can be held responsible for inadequacies while any possible credit accrues to oneself" (Boguslaw, 1968, p. 59). The scientist must believe in his own findings with utter conviction while doubting those of others with all his worth (Mitroff, 1974b).

The themes of this chapter should be taken more in the spirit of a challenge rather than as conclusions. The challenge is to understand more fully what a Feeling science would look like by actively working to bring it about. We can begin to see what such a science would be like. Among other things, a Feeling science would not be afraid to display an ever-present, underlying emotional basis beneath an apparently impersonal, logical, and rational surface structure of science. Science can no longer afford to deny its emotional foundations.

Another way to. put the matter is that the notion of a feeling-based science undercuts one of the most central cultural assumptions of conventional science—the cultural presupposition of masculinity. As Maslow (1966) and others have pointed out, conventional science is strongly masculine in its orientation, reflecting traditional and stereotypical male values: it is "hard-nosed," objective, value-free; it eschews the ambiguous, the speculative, the vague, the beautiful, and the good. A feminine science in contrast is not afraid of the good, the speculative, the vague, or the unique; indeed, it courts them, openly confronts them, and makes positive virtues of them.

We certainly do not contend that men can do science and women cannot. Rather, what we are saying is that much of our science is built on stereotypical concepts of masculinity.

Mitroff, Jacob, and Moore (1977) recently performed a study of the spouses of physical scientists in order to find out if the spouses (male as well as female) paid any price or reaped any benefits from the fact of their mate being a scientist. Does conventional science—with its emphasis on emotional neutrality—exact an unusual cost from its active participants (scientists themselves) and its behind-the-scene supporters (their spouses)? Spouses in numerous other occupational groups have been studied in this regard (see Helfrich, 1965; Kanter, 1977). The fact that these questions have not been addressed in science is telling evidence in itself. Have we been afraid to look at the personal side of science because of what that might tell us about science and ourselves? We believe so.

In the study of scientists' spouses, fourteen married couples were interviewed: fourteen male scientists, eight female scientists, and six female nonscientists. (Most male and female scientists were in the field of high-energy physics.) All twenty-eight respondents were asked to fill out five semantic differentials (SDs) which rated Adult Man (M), Adult Woman (F), Scientist (S), Yourself, and Your Spouse against twelve scales. The scales were chosen from a larger set of forty-one scales devised by Broverman and others (1972) to rate the five SD concepts for male and female stereotypes.

One-way analyses of variance (ANOVA) on each scale revealed that in ten cases out of twelve there were significant differences between the concepts being rated. Indeed, on eight scales there were highly significant differences ($p < 0.005$). One pattern in particular is pertinent to our discussion. With the exception of two scales out of twelve, the concepts S, M, and F were aligned not only in that order (S to M to F) but in order of increasing masculinity. The concept of the scientist is perceived as more masculine than the Adult Man, which in turn is perceived as more masculine than the Adult Woman.

The question raised by the PH is: Can we really suppose our science to have remained immune from such influences? If not, then the challenge is to develop a methodology of science that does justice not only to the humanity of our subjects but to us as investigators. Roe (1961, p. 457) sums up the need for this undertaking: "I think many scientists are genuinely unaware of the extent or the fact of involvement [in their work] and themselves accept the myth of impersonal objectivity. This is really very unfortunate. It is true that only a man who is passionately involved in his work is likely to make important contributions, but the committed man who knows he is committed and can come to terms with this fact has a good chance of getting beyond his commitment and of learning how to disassociate himself from his idea when this is necessary. There is little in the traditional education of scientists to prepare them for this necessity as there are many who are still unaware of it."

As we train scientists to depersonalize and form abstract generalizations, perhaps we should also train them to adopt the style of the ethnographer and to personalize their accounts.

SEVEN

Systemic Knowledge: An Integrated Science

It has been put to me that one should in fact distinguish carefully between science as a body of knowledge, science as what scientists do and science as a social institution. This is precisely the sort of distinction that one must not *make. . . .* The problem has been to discover a unifying principle for science in all its aspects [*emphasis added*]. *Before one can distinguish separately the philosophical, psychological, or sociological dimensions of science, one must somehow have succeeded in characterizing it as a whole.*

John Ziman (1968, pp. 11–12)

It is our hope in this final chapter to place the issues we have been discussing within the broader context of the field of science; to illustrate, via two holistic or systemic models, the interdependence between the four views of scientific methodology we have discussed; and to show what unification of the different viewpoints entails— the prospects for and the difficulties standing in the way of change in the institution of science.

In recent years, there has been growing criticism of the separation between the philosophy and the sociology of science (Barnes and Dolby, 1970; Churchman, 1968, 1971; Mitroff, 1974a; Phillips, 1974). Briefly, the criticism is that while the separation has been comforting to philosophers and sociologists alike in relieving them of the burden of having to understand each other's knowledge and concerns, one cannot properly study or understand the social-institutional system of science independent of its cognitive-intellectual structure.

We contend that the entire field of science is in need of revolution and revision—not just the philosophy and the sociology of science—and we are critical of all distinctions and divisions that separate the history, philosophy, psychology, sociology, and methodology of science from one another. Anything less than a systemic or holistic approach will fail to capture and do justice to the phenomenon of science.

In the following sections we present a brief survey of the major concerns that have characterized the history, philosophy, psychology, and sociology of science and divided them from one another. Recent empirical studies and theoretical criticisms indicate that these variables and concerns actually presuppose and depend on one another. Thus any apparent opposition in the various fields of science is dialectic in nature, because the variables of one field are defined as much by what they exclude and are opposed to as by what they are in harmony with and include.

We also present a systems model for the study and understanding of science which includes two important subsystems of science: the epistemic or problem-solving structure of science and the social, political, and organizational structure of science. The two submodels continually interact and presuppose one another and show precisely where each of the four viewpoints of science discussed in previous chapters enters into the total system of science.

Selective Map of Scientific Studies

The following pages present a list of the major contemporary works in the philosophy, history, sociology, and psychology of science. We do not mean to imply that the list is exhaustive or that every author fits neatly into a single disciplinary area. Indeed, there are a number of important thinkers whose work cuts across more than one category. In classifying the studies, our major criterion was the intellectual tradition or discipline out of which the work seemed to emanate.

Certain conclusions emerge from this list, and we believe they are not merely artifacts of our categorization. For example, the tradition represented by the category "philosophy of science" is, with the exception of Polanyi, identified exclusively with the logic of science. The primary emphases are on: (1) the logical character and representation of scientific theories; (2) a rigid distinction between the "soft," unorderly processes of discovering a theory and the "hard," orderly processes of testing it; (3) a clear separation between unproblematic, "public" observations and problematic, hypothetical theories; and (4) a clear demarcation between the application of social psychology (to discovery) and logic of science (to testing) along with the assumption of the general superiority of logic over social psychology.

Everything that the philosophy of science (logic) has asserted as characteristic of science has been denied by the history of science in the form of a countercharacteristic. Little wonder the tension between these two areas has been so great. For instance, where logic has stressed the logical character of science, the history of science has delighted in showing the alogical and illogical nature of actual scientific practice. It does little good to say that logic is concerned with the characteristics of science as an ideal system of knowledge whereas history is concerned with studying science as it is. An ideal method, after all, must bear some relation to feasibility; otherwise we may not just be pursuing an ideal world but a fantasy world (Maxwell, 1972).

Major Fields of Science Studies Classified by Investigators, Major Substantive Ideas and Critical Distinctions Introduced

Philosophy of Science

Reichenbach (1968) introduction of critical disjunction between contexts of discovery and testing.

Feigl (1970) elaboration of the orthodox or "received" view of scientific theories (primitive terms, uninterpreted observational base, formal theoretical language, deduction of consequences); disjunction between theoretical and observational entities.

Hempel (1965, 1970) studies in the logic of explanation; covering-law model of scientific theories; deductive character of scientific explanation.

Nagel (1961) logical character of scientific laws.

Popper (1965, 1970) emphasis on falsification as the distinctive character of scientific knowledge; strong demarcation between the social-psychology and logic of science on basis of emphasis on distinction between contexts of discovery and testing; strong assertion of superiority of logic of science over social psychology, emphasis on asymmetry between verification and falsification; critique of psychologism and sociologism.

Scheffler (1967, 1972) strong critique of Kuhn; re-emphasis on nonrelativistic, neutral character of scientific data as impartial arbiters of theories.

Caws (1969) discovery as no less "logical" in character than testing.

Polanyi (1964) the personal character of scientific knowledge, the tacit dimension.

History of Science

Duhem (1954) emphasis on inconclusive nature of scientific experiments; impossibility of a crucial falsifying experiment in science.

Hanson (1965, 1969, 1970) emphasis on virtual inseparability of all observations and theory; discovery as patterned and theory-laden.

Kuhn (1962) Normal and Revolutionary science; scientific paradigms; interaction between theory and data; emphasis on social-historical character of science; bad side-effects of the pedagogy of science (the textbook).

Feyerabend (1975) severe critique of the logical, rule-patterned accounts of science as a "rational" process; emphasis on the irrational, anarchistic, subjective, idiosyncratic features; emphasis on theory-ladenness of all observation; need for incommensurable theories.

Holton (1973, 1974) role of conflicting themata in science; interaction between "public" and "private" science; tolerance of ambiguity and conflicting themata as a prime characteristic of the great scientists; case studies of Einstein.

Westfall (1973) case studies of Newton's "fudge factoring" subjective behavior.

Price (1969) growth of scientific journals, societies; demographic studies of science.

King (1971) historical critique of the Mertonian norms of science.

Ravetz (1971) the social problems and context of scientific knowledge.

Lakatos (1970) critique of Popperian naive falsificationism; protection of theories from falsificationism: protection of theories from premature testing.

Toulmin (1972) critique of "logicism"; critique of externalist-internalist distinction.

Sociology of Science

Merton (1938, 1942, 1961, 1968, 1969) studies of seventeenth century science, societies; formulation of the norms of science; analysis of priority races; the ambivalence of scientists; sociology of knowledge.

Zuckerman (1967, 1970) reward system of science; study of Nobel prize winners.

Crane (1969, 1972) study of the gate-keeping function in science; invisible colleges.

Hagstrom (1965) social structure of different fields of science.

Cole (1967, 1970) citation structure of science.

Mullins (1972, 1973) structure of different scientific specialties; theory groups in sociology.

Barnes and Dolby (1970) critique of Mertonian norms of science.

Mulkay (1969, 1972) critique of Mertonian norms; function of scientific theories as norms.

Lodahl and Gordon (1972) structure of different scientific fields; levels of paradigmatic development.

Psychology of Science

Roe (1951, 1953, 1954, 1961) psychological portraits of scientists in different disciplines via traditional clinical instruments, (projective) background data, origins of, childhood interests, religious interests.

Eiduson (1962, 1973) in-depth interviews with scientists, family backgrounds.

Kubie (1954, 1961) psychoanalytic analysis of the problems of the scientific career role.

McClelland (1970) in-depth summary of work of Roe; studies of the imagery of scientists.

Hudson (1966) studies of differences between arts and science students, diverger/converger distinction; spouses of scientists.

Maslow (1966) analysis of the conflicting psychological elements inherent in the scientific method, rigidity, compulsiveness—fear of the unstructured and unknown versus openness—playfulness; ability to suspend structure and welcome the unknown.

Mitroff (1974a,b) psychological analysis of different scientific roles; projective images of physical objects; extreme aggressiveness of science; spouses of scientists; characterization of working epistemologies and norms-in-use.

Garvey (1971) structure of the communication system of science.

Simon (1973) analyses of science as a complex problem-solving activity; justification for the heuristic character of a "logic" of discovery.

In a similar vein, there is rarely any clear division between the discovery and testing phases of scientific inquiry but rather a continual crossing over and interaction of the two. Indeed, powerful arguments have been advanced against the need for such a distinction at all (Feyerabend, 1975). By the same token, the lack of a clear separation between observations and theories has also been stressed (Hanson, 1965, 1969). In fact, it has been suggested that observations are not neutral at all, but theory laden. This means that we can only collect scientific observations by presupposing some theory about the phenomenon under study, and the presumption of different theories is likely to give rise to different observations (as we have stressed in Chapter Four).

Scientific historians lack consensus primarily with regard to the status of the sociology and psychology of science. Kuhn (1962) is sympathetic to both psychology and sociology and relies heavily upon them in fashioning a theory of science. Feyerabend and Hanson have likewise utilized psychology in their own approaches.

Toulmin (1972), in contrast, argues that science cannot be understood in terms of a set of fixed rational rules but must instead be understood in terms of "evolutionary" processes. That is, while espousing a cultural point of view, Toulmin adopts a biological explanatory base rather than a sociological or psychological one.

The psychology of science has remained relatively independent of the traditions represented in the foregoing list. With the notable exception of Simon's (1973) essay on the "heuristic lawlike" character of discovery, the psychology of science has stood apart from the issue that has occupied logicians and historians of science—the structure of scientific knowledge—emphasizing instead the personalities, family origins, religious backgrounds, and so forth of scientists. With the exception of works by Maslow (1966), Mitroff (1974b), and Simon (1973), there has been little study from a psychological point of view of science as a particular subject matter. This may be partly because the psychology of science as a formal field of study is the least developed and institutionalized of all the research traditions.

The relationship between the history and the sociology of science has been asymmetrical in that the history of science seems more willing to adopt a sociological perspective in its approach to historical analysis than the sociology of science seems willing to borrow concepts from history (with the notable exception of Merton, 1957, 1961). This is certainly reflected in the contemporary sociology of science, which emphasizes (1) science as a social institution governed by universal norms of social systems (Storer, 1966); (2) the reward and allocation system of science which favors some scientists more than others; and (3) the social structure of different subgroups of scientists. The primary emphasis, in other words, is on the social structure of science independent of how that structure affects the generation of scientific knowledge. With the exception of Mulkay (1969, 1972) there has been little mention, and even less empirical study, of how the substantive subject matter of science can give rise to the social norms of science, and vice versa.

Our list of areas of scientific endeavor is also helpful in what it does *not* show—that is, what has not been studied in depth. In the language of analysis of variance, each of the major traditions represented has tended to study "main effects." (A main effect is a study of variables solely *within* a single tradition; it would not relate variables across different fields.) What is lacking is a comprehensive study of interaction effects. Examples of what some possible interaction effects and questions might look like is given in Table 6, which attempts to portray what each field potentially has to contribute to the others by making possible the study of a unique interaction effect. The history of science is represented by the intersection of the history row and column. (Note that our earlier listing of areas of science contains the diagonal cells of the matrix—only a small proportion of possible studies.)

Following Lazarsfeld (personal communication) we adopt the following convention for reading the matrix. We consider each discipline both a potential donor and recipient of the substantive knowledge, concerns, and methods of each of the others. We are considering here only 2 × 2 interaction effects; that is, the interaction of only two fields at a time, rather than the simultaneous interaction of three or four areas with each other. Thus we are only touching the surface of the phenomenon of science. The full understanding of science as a total system demands that we understand how the historical, philosophical, psychological, and sociological elements of science all act in simultaneous conjunction with one another.

We are not implying that there has been no study at all of two-way effects. For instance, Manuel's (1968) psychoanalytic portrait of Newton stands as a notable example of the psycho-history approach. Likewise, the cells labeled "historico-philosophy" and "philosophical history" represent questions being confronted by the newly emerging discipline of the history and philosophy of science. In fact, the tradition labeled "History of Science" in the list of major fields of scientific studies exhibits, on closer inspection, the boldest excursion into the region of interaction effects. Thus, the work of Thomas Kuhn (1962) represents the importation of sociological analysis and reasoning into the field of history. The work of Hanson (1965, 1969, 1970) likewise stands out as an excellent example of the sophisticated use of psychological concepts in historical analysis.

To summarize, we contend that the interaction questions have not been as consistently and self-consciously studied as the

Table 6. A matrix of some possible studies of science formed by pairwise interaction effects of disciplinary traditions.

	Philosophy	History	Psychology	Sociology
Philosophy		PHILOSOPHICAL HISTORY OF SCIENCE Is it possible to build a model of science that would satisfy both the philosopher and the historian of science? What would a dialectical treatment of scientific history look like?	PHILOSOPHICAL PSYCHOLOGY OF SCIENCE What is the evidential status for the existences of different types of scientists? How does the existence of different types bear on the creation and validation of scientific knowledge? What would an appropriate logic be for adjudicating the conflicting claims of different scientists?	PHILOSOPHICAL SOCIOLOGY OF SCIENCE Are the norms of science necessary, sufficient? How do social norms bear on scientific knowledge? Is there a disjunction between social norms and scientific theories? Can theories function as norms? Are norms organized into opposing dialectical sets? What would an appropriate logic be for adjudicating conflicting norms? Should one be more severe in testing one's opponents?
History	HISTORICO-PHILOSOPHY OF SCIENCE What would a logical reconstruction of science look like that was grounded in the realities of historical practice? Is a logical account possible that incorporates the irrationality and nonrationality of science, as well as changing concepts of rationality? Is it necessary to presuppose timeless standards of rationality?		HISTORICO-PSYCHOLOGY OF SCIENCE Does history suggest a richer and broader set of labels and concepts for classifying different types of scientists? How does the historical context help us in understanding individual scientific personalities? Is there a constancy of different types through different periods? Is personality a response to the period, or vice versa?	HISTORICO-SOCIOLOGY OF SCIENCE Are norms invariant? Do they change over time? Has the interaction between science and the larger society always been the same? Can we use history to give us better categories for contemporary surveys of scientists?

PSYCHOLOGY OF SCIENTIFIC KNOWLEDGE:

Do different psychological types have different concepts of rationality, objectivity, logics of discovery and testing, methodologies of science; of science itself? Is a psycho-logic of science possible? Do all types equally accept the distinctions between discovery and testing, observations and theory? Can we build a simulation model of the inner workings of science? What is the role of different types in scientific knowledge? Is a healthy science possible? Does the growth of science necessitate neuroticism?

PSYCHO-HISTORY OF SCIENCE:

What would a definition of a paradigm be that did not presuppose consensus? In what sense are the physical sciences in a pre-paradigmatic stage? Can we use clinical methods to form a psychological portrait of scientists from historical documents? Can we study the psychological forces behind the origin and growth of modern science? How does psychology help us in understanding the historical context of science? Is the historical context a response to the personalities of scientists or vice versa?

PSYCHO-SOCIOLOGY OF SCIENCE

Do different types have different norms? Does a particular psychology stand behind different norms? Do different types exhibit a differential degree of migration into and out of various disciplines? Is there a particular psychological orientation that is similar to elite scientists? Are there personality differences between fields?

SOCIOLOGY OF SCIENTIFIC KNOWLEDGE:

Do different social groups of scientists have different concepts of rationality, objectivity, etc.? Do groups differ in the amount of protection time they are willing to give to a new theory before subjecting it to crucial tests? What are the functional/dysfunctional consequences of having different group concepts of science? Are groups more severe in testing the claims of their competitors than those of their friends?

SOCIO-HISTORY OF SCIENCE:

Can historical documents be read as social surveys which give us a sociological analysis of the times? To what extent can sociometric techniques be used to understand the group structure of scientific societies? Can the attitudes of elites versus nonelites be discerned from past records? Can the origin of paradigms be inferred by social techniques?

SOCIAL PSYCHOLOGY OF SCIENCE

To what extent do institutional forces shape different personality types? To what extent do the norms of science shape types? What would an appropriate set of projective tests look like for getting at the unconscious institutional features of science?

main effect questions. We see, for example, little current demand for such hybrid disciplines as "the psychology of scientific knowledge." The larger the number of interactions, the less systematic study it has received: the number of simultaneously combined studies in the philosophy, psychology, and sociology of science is virtually nil.

We turn now to an elaboration of two submodels of a larger model of science. The submodels will allow us not only to tie together some of the preceding points but also to demonstrate some of the higher-order interaction effects that were merely alluded to above.

Toward a Systems Model of Science

In previous papers (Mitroff, 1977; Mitroff and Turoff, 1974), we have discussed some of the properties of a deceptively simple submodel of the epistemic or problem-solving structure of science. Here we will emphasize higher-order interaction effects with regard to the four viewpoints of scientific methodology discussed in Chapters Three through Six.

Figure 3 portrays the main qualitative features of the model. Suppose that every scientific inquiry starts with the extreme left-hand circle, the "felt existence" or recognition of a problem situation—what a naive realist would be inclined to call Reality but what a pragmatist like Dewey (1953) labeled the Problematic Situation. From the point of view of systems thinking, there are no simple starting or ending points in the process of inquiry. One can begin as well as end the process at any point in the model. Indeed, where one starts and ends is a complicated function of the development of one's field of science (history), the social organization of the discipline (sociology), one's preferred methodology (philosophy), and one's personality type (psychology). Where one starts and ends an inquiry results in a complicated four-way interaction effect. The starting and ending points are not only potential candidates for explication by all four research traditions, but it is doubtful whether they could be entirely explained by any of the four major fields of science studies acting in isolation.

The path from Problem Situation to Conceptual Model indicates that if one enters the system at Problem Situation then the

Figure 3: A Systems View of Problem Solving

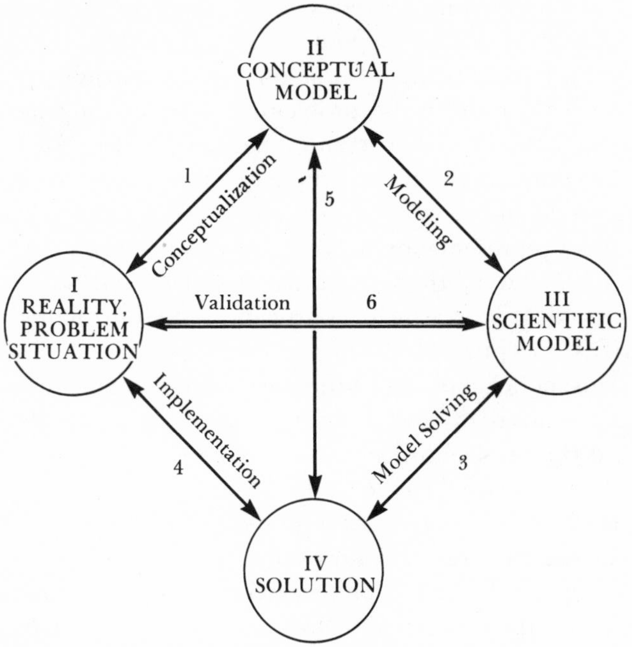

first phase of problem solving consists in formulating a Conceptual Model of the problem—defining the problem in the most basic and broadest terms; that is, from a macro perspective, not from an exact, detailed, micro one. For example, the Conceptual Model specifies whether the problem is one of physics, chemistry, economics, psychology, and so forth. If the problem is one of physical mechanics, then the model determines whether it is a problem in classical mechanics or relativistic mechanics. The choice of a Conceptual Model is akin to the choice of a world view (Pepper, 1942)—indicative of a deep commitment to a particular view of reality. Differences among different fields and traditions can be especially severe. Indeed, we believe it is this level that Kuhn (1962) and Hanson (1965, 1969) had in mind when they claimed that the proponents of different traditions literally "see different realities."

Once a Conceptual Model has been chosen, consciously or unconsciously, a detailed and precise Scientific Model can be formed and a Solution derived from it. If the Scientific Model is mathematical, then the Solution (if one is possible) will be formally derived. If the Scientific Model is empirical, then the Solution will be an empirically testable hypothesis. If the Solution is finally fed back to the initial Problem Situation for the purpose of taking action on it (to remove the problem), we have Implementation, which constitutes the action-taking phase of problem solving.

To complete the model, the path from Reality to Scientific Model corresponds to the "degree of correspondence" between reality and a representation or model of reality (Hesse, 1966). The vertical path between the Conceptual Model and the Solution represents the degree to which a particular Solution follows from a particular Conceptual Model and vice versa.

This model explicates a number of fundamental matters regarding the nature of science. Each phase of the model potentially involves different scientific norms (ideologies), different standards of rationality and performance, different psychological types, linguistic levels of analysis, and the paradigmatic development of a particular science. Consider, for example, the matter of linguistics. The Conceptual Modeling phase obviously involves questions of semantics, for the concern at this level is with the basic meaning of the Problematic Situation and its representation within an appropriate universe of discourse. The Scientific Modeling phase involves matters of syntax. The Solution phase involves testing and development and is therefore a matter of empirics. The concern of both these phases is with the detailed and valid manipulation of concepts within some formalized language. The semantic concern is the choice between two or more competing languages for conceptualizing a problem; the syntactical and empirical concerns work within a particular chosen language structure. Finally, the Implementation phase involves matters of pragmatics: Does the proposed theoretical solution work in practice? Does it make a difference?

These same stages elucidate the various competing standards of rationality operating throughout the model. Syntactic rationality (both technical and empirical) is concerned with questions such as: Does effect x follow precisely and impersonally from antecedent condition y? Semantic rationality asks whether a particular problem makes sense or is interesting to a particular audience

(Davis, 1971). In the same vein, pragmatic rationality asks how and whether the theoretical Solution measures up in the context of practice.

Above all, the model helps to make clear why the distinction between the logic and the social psychology of research (see Popper, 1965; Reichenbach, 1968) fails to hold upon closer inspection. Current research (Gordon and others, 1974) is beginning to show that different psychological types are better suited for some of the phases of the model than for others. This implies that the epistemic structure functions effectively only because there is an effective social allocation function of the different types to the different phases. The system as a whole can function effectively only if the epistemic structure is in tune with the social psychological structure, and vice versa.

At this point we can see precisely where our four different methodologies of science fit into the larger system model of scientific inquiry represented in the major fields list. The Conceptual Modeling Phase is the domain of the CT and CH. The fundamental difference between them is that whereas the CT stresses the analytical, impersonal features of reality, the CH stresses the personal, human features. Both, however, are concerned with posing significant semantic questions, whether or not they can be asked or answered with the precision of the AS.

The AS is best suited for the Scientific Modeling and Solution phases of inquiry. Here precision and lack of ambiguity are appropriate criteria, but the AS goes too far if he or she insists that they are appropriate everywhere.

Finally, the PH is best suited to the implementation phases of research. Working with individuals, organizations, interpersonal relationships, and issues of timing are very important here. The PH's forte is extreme sensitivity to these issues.

Given the placement of the different methodological types on the model, we can appreciate the lack of communication and concomitant opposition between them: Each is attuned to different phases of the inquiry process. Each wishes to take the favored phase out of context and make it the privileged focal point of inquiry. However, as we can see from Figure 3, each phase is only part of the total picture. Each depends upon the others. It makes no sense to ask which is more important, for all presuppose one another. Each issue is at some point indebted to previous inquiries for conceptual model building, scientific model, and so on. Instead of fighting one another, they should learn to appreciate one another.

To give a concrete illustration, consider the matter of questionnaire design. The AS would begin by giving a proposed set of items to as large a population as possible in order to ascertain whether the items are each individually and jointly discriminating enough and would be concerned with the test-retest reliability of the items and scales in the questionnaire. He would also be interested in the technical validity of the questionnaire as measured by one of several precise notions of technical validity. Thus, in order for a questionnaire to be valid for the AS, it would have to adhere to some rather precise and rigorous methodological standards.

One of the major differences between the AS and the CT is that whereas the AS uses a questionnaire to test already formulated hypotheses, the CT uses a questionnaire to develop new ideas. A recent study by Mitroff (1974b) demonstrates this difference quite vividly. In a semantic differential (SD) questionnaire, about a third of the respondents, because of the complexity of the concept being rated, wanted to place multiple checks on several of the scales, which would have interfered with the usual forms of statistical analyses. The experimenter had to decide whether to allow the respondents to make multiple checks or insist on a single check per scale. The issue was the object and extent of control. Should responses be controlled by the standard format of administering the SD or should the actual responses be allowed to surface and hence to control the instrument? Mitroff allowed the actual responses to rule in this case even though it was anticipated that this would create difficulties in the statistical analyses, and by so doing allowed some interesting findings to emerge.

The setting in which the SD was given also illustrates the CH and PH approaches. SDs were handed out personally to each subject. Thus, in addition to securing impersonal check marks on the scales, Mitroff also gathered valuable verbal protocols which were tape recorded for later content analysis. The qualitative patterns gathered in this way allowed an interesting CH approach to structured questionnaires to emerge. In effect, as each subject "talked through" each scale, each scale served as a projective test. Indeed, the subjects were strongly encouraged to verbalize their reactions to each scale. In this way both qualitative and quantitative data were collected, each of which enhanced the meaning of the other.

PH aspects also emerge from this design. A number of the subjects told very personal stories about themselves and their close colleagues. The technique individuated the subjects and the concept they were rating (the Ideal Scientist).

Science as an Institutional System

Needless to say, Figure 3 does not exhaust all the relevant features of science considered as a total system. It is merely intended as a micromodel of the epistemic structure of science without reference to how the epistemic structure influences and is influenced by the environment in which it exists. For example, it does not illustrate where the publication and review process enters in.

Figure 4 is a macromodel derived from the field of organizational behavior (Kilmann and Mitroff, 1977) but can be equally applied to the institution of science. This Analytical Model of Institutions is drawn from the field of organizational behavior because science does not function in a political and social vacuum: the broader aspects of science are both institutional and political.

The first aspect of the model to be considered is the distinction between an open and a closed system. One of the major contributions of management science and organization theory has been the recognition that an organization is highly dependent on its environment for a variety of resources such as information and inputs as well as ultimately an outlet for its products or services (Maurer, 1971). Several decades ago most theories assumed that the organization was a closed system, and virtually all research concerned the internal functioning of the organization (Gulick and Urwick, 1937). At that time, the environment of most organizations was, in fact, fairly stable; there were no major changes in technology, information, or societal needs. In the past few decades, however, the environments of organizations have become more dynamic than ever before. The Analytical Model of Institu-

Figure 4: A Macro Model of Science—the Analytical Model of Institutions

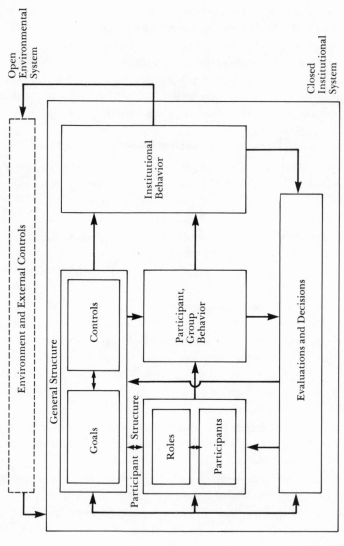

tions takes this into account by drawing around institutional activity a boundary which indicates the points at which the environment needs to be monitored and how the environment influences the functioning of the institution. The actual boundary that defines the institutional system (vis-a-vis its environment) is determined by those variables that the organization can control over the short run. Thus, the selection of scientists (participants), the socialization of scientists to norms and procedures as the "scientific method" (roles), the long-term and short-term goals of science, and the mechanism to assure the attainment of these goals (that is, controls such as reviews for publication and other "reward" systems) can be directly altered by those inside the scientific institution. However, several variables cannot be immediately or directly controlled by the institution and are classified as environmental variables. They include: the basic economic condition in the nation, the political-legal structure, the availability of certain technologies, and the general culture. At an intermediate level, environmental variables include other institutions (the family, church, funding agencies, industrial organizations). Finally, at the microlevel of analysis, environmental variables include individual members of society who may eventually use scientific knowledge. All of these environmental variables can be confronted and changed in the long run; for example, lobby groups like The American Association for the Advancement of Science affect political issues, research develops new technologies, and education affects culture. The concepts and variables that are generally most attuned to self-regulation, however, are those within the institution that are subject to change in the short run.

The next structure of the institution illustrated by the model is goals and controls. The goals specify what the institution expects to accomplish: what knowledge or services it will provide, which other institutions it seeks to serve, and what general resources it will apply to the solution of certain social problems. The controls specify the basic method or design by which the institution will attempt to achieve these goals: disciplinary divisions, selection policies, socialization policies, reward and incentive systems, and other institutional policies (such as ethics) to guide decision making on scientific affairs. The general structure of goals and controls is thus the blueprint of the institution, stating what to accomplish and how, even if only the level of broad policy guidelines and broad design categories of resources.

The environment of the institution has an influence on the goals and controls possible and available to the institution (note the arrow). First, the goals are realistic only if they address some problem in the environment and if the institution can command the necessary resources, expertise, and design to approach these goals. Second, there are often legal and moral constraints on the institution which preclude the use of certain control mechanisms. In science, for example, there are moral and legal restrictions on the use of human subjects in experiments. The effect of the environment on the institution's general structure becomes most noticeable when the institution applies its goals and controls to "new" scientific fields (such as the social sciences in the twentieth century) within the same general structure as the more established fields such as physics—only to find that the old structure does not apply to the new fields. The nature of phenomena and their "environments" are different, requiring a different general structure for treating them.

The general structure by itself, however, is not enough to foster effective institutional behavior. For one thing, more specific guidelines need to be developed so that each subdivision and individual in the institution knows what is expected, how and with whom to interact, who is evaluating performance on what criteria, what specific methodologies and recourses are to be utilized, and so forth. This requires a participant structure which divides the general structure into specific behaviors through which the institution and its subparts function; in science these are the disciplines and the subspecialties. Each participant in the institution is thus given a role, which can be fairly specific (as in the case of formal scientific method) or merely a set of expectations regarding the participant's contributions to the institution. The concept of role can be further divided into two components: programmed versus discretionary. The former contains specific prescriptions while the latter recognizes that not all of an individual's behavior can be determined beforehand and that the institution must allow for some freedom and discretion. When the phenomenon under study is fairly complex and changing, the role naturally cannot be heavily programmed; if the phenomenon is well structured, the role can be relatively programmed.

The concept of participants designates not simply the person but also the various characteristics of the person relevant to institutional performance (skills, values, experience, needs, and so on) upon which each participant can be assessed. The concept of role includes attribution of the task, required skills, assumed values of scientific behavior, and expected patterns of interaction with participants in other institutional roles. Also important is the fit between the participant and the role: To what extent are the person's skills congruent with the skill requirement of the task? Is the nature of the work consistent with the individual's needs for self-expression? It can be a serious mistake to place a PH type in a position requiring CT attributes or skills.

The environment of the institution also has a direct influence on the participant structure. The roles in the institution are only functional if they prescribe expected behavior that can actually be performed by participants. However, in some cases participants with the necessary skills may not be available either inside or outside the institution. There may also be certain norms in society which preclude certain tasks and jobs from being defined within role descriptions. Furthermore, there may be legislation which forbids the institution to define a role as relevant to only a certain class of people (for example, white male scientists). Thus, although matching certain roles and participants may be desirable from an institution's point of view (for example, previous selection and training of male scientists), the environment may require the institution to operate by a broader set of objectives (anti-discrimination).

In the analytical model of institutions, the behavior that is actually observed within the institution is referred to as participant and group behavior. This includes people working on tasks, interacting with one another—in short "concrete behavior." Participant and group behavior actually represent unconceptualized behavior. However, to understand what is causing the observed behavior, one must hypothesize various forces or influences. The model indicates that participant and group behavior are determined by the general structure and the participant structure of the institution (goals, controls, roles, and participants) as well as influences from the environment. The reason people in the institution behave in certain ways is based on the general goals of the institution and the control mechanisms set up to pursue these goals. In addition, each participant has been selected according to some criteria for skills, values, and other characteristics and is given a role which will specifically guide his behavior in the pursuit of more general scientific goals. In other words, the concepts involved in the general structure and participant structure of the institution are those that have been hypothesized as determining (or at least influencing) behavior in the institution.

Institutional behavior is a separate category and is distinguished from participant and group behavior in that the latter are observed vis-à-vis the internal functioning of the institution while institutional behavior is observed vis-à-vis the environment of the institution. Often there may be a discrepancy between internal and external perceptions of behavior, which may be a manifestation of certain institutional problems. For example, institutions often foster a particular public image which may or may not be in line with how the institution is actually functioning or how scientific knowledge is actually being developed. In Figure 4, an arrow goes from the participant and group behavior box to the institution behavior box, signifying that one influences the other. Another arrow goes from institutional behavior to the environment of the institution, signifying that institutions can and do influence their broader environment (illustrated by the recent growing concern for ethics and social responsibility), although the effect is not always as direct and powerful as the environmental influence on the institution. In general, the environment consists of many more resources than the institution and therefore the environment is more powerful, unless several institutions combine, either implicitly or explicitly, to affect the environment.

An important element of any conceptual model is one that specifically allows individuals, change agents, or problem solvers to enter the model in order to assess the institution and then to make changes to solve a problem situation. This element is contained within the box labeled "Evaluation and Decision Making."

The basic inputs to evaluation and decision making are participant and group behavior, institutional behavior, and the environment of the institution, which are introduced by quantitative or qualitative measures of behavior and outcomes of internal and external activities. Usually the institution has a formal measure of outcome variables—for instance, new scientific developments and findings. In addition, the institution may have some measures of group behavior, such as the accomplishments of various disciplines and subdisciplines. Most institutions also have some formal assessment of environmental variables: economic trends, technological needs, political developments, and so forth. Furthermore, institutions develop informal qualitative measures of various processes and outcomes which may be too inconvenient or costly to represent quantitatively. For example, organizations such as the National Science Foundation have been exploring sophisticated management information systems to consider systematically what kinds of information are necessary to make various management decisions.

The model is intended to show that the general structure and the participant structure of the institution are the prime determinants of participant, group, and institutional behavior. Consequently, any discrepancy between goals and performance can be conceptually traced to the goals, controls, roles, and participants and their interactions within the institution and between the institution and its environment; therefore, solution of some problem situation requires a change in these basic concepts. More specifically, a discrepancy between goals and performance may be because goals were set too high, because the institution's overall control mechanisms have not been effective (the design of disciplines is not conducive to high performance; the reward system does not appropriately guide members; and so on), or because the interaction between goals and controls is inconsistent and mutually constraining. For example, scientific goals may emphasize the greater utilization of scientific knowledge while reward systems foster new theoretical research.

The source of the discrepancies between goals and performance may also be defined vis-à-vis the participants in the institution: they may lack the expertise, training, and motivation to perform effectively. Alternatively, it may be that the roles are ill-defined and do not correctly specify the work to be done or the resources to be utilized. The interaction between roles and participants may be the source of the problem: participants may have the necessary expertise, roles may be appropriately defined, but the matching between participants and roles may have been ineffective—the right people may be working in the wrong roles.

A source of a problem situation might also be in the interaction between the general structure and the participant structure—how well the institution has translated its general, long-term plans into its short-term activities. The general structure may reflect the good intentions of the institution but the overall participant structure may no longer effectively implement these intentions, or the participant structure may be effective but the general structure may be outmoded and no longer provide a useful framework of long-term direction for short-term activities.

Finally, the analytical model of institutions suggests that the environment itself may be a source of discrepancy between goals and performance. For example, attitudes towards science may have changed, thus affecting the possibilities of goal attainment, norms for working, or attitudes regarding the use of scientific knowledge. While the institution may not be able to affect its environment directly, a change in goals may do so indirectly since different segments of the environment become pertinent to the institution as goals are changed.

The foregoing concepts and interactions are all possible sources of the institution's problem situation and are therefore potential sources of resolution of the problems. While it is beyond the scope of this book to indicate the full range of institutional problems, we can at least touch on the following considerations: In general, it is more costly and difficult to change the goals and controls in the general structure than elements of the participant structure. Changes in goals and controls, because of their centrality to the institution, send ripples throughout the rest of the system; they require changes in the roles and participants, since the latter implement and thus further define the former. However, changes in roles and participants do not necessarily require changes in the general structure since roles and participants are more specific.

Basically, the more pervasive the change and the number of other variables that are affected by the change, the more institutions tend to resist the change. This resistance protects the status quo of individuals, positions, attitudes, spheres of influence, and so forth. Thus, the change that has the greatest effect in the institution, such as a change in the general structure of scientific disciplines, is also least likely to be enacted; the change that has the least effect on the institution, that is, in the participant structure, is most apt to be applied (for example, more stringent selection methods).

What the model illuminates most of all is the central theme of this chapter—the strong interaction between the so-called separate aspects of science and the separate disciplines which study those aspects. For example, one can approach the goals of science from the perspective of each of the listed four major fields of science studies. The philosophy of science (Maxwell, 1972) has claimed that the goal of science is to increase the logical and empirical content of our theories about the world—that is, to maximize scientific truth. The history of science has the goal of furthering the evolution of scientific truth and rationality and broadening the definition of these terms (Toulmin, 1972). The psychology of science has the goal of developing noncompulsive, healthy scientists and a psychologically "healthy" concept of science itself (Maslow, 1966). Finally, the sociology of science has the goal of developing the rational allocation and assignment of the most qualified individuals to the social roles to which they are most suited (Merton and Zuckerman, 1973).

A similar point could be made with respect to the norms of science as they are defined by the four traditions. From the standpoint of social psychology, scientific norms are manifested in the specific roles that scientists assume; as a result of occupying these roles, scientists come to internalize the norms of science (Mitroff, 1974a, 1974b). However, a more interesting point follows directly from the model itself. As control mechanisms vary (depending on the size, location, and immediacy of a particular project), one would expect that the norms of science would also vary; it is not expected that one would apply the same scientific norms to one's immediate colleagues as to one's remote colleagues and competitors (Mitroff, 1974a, 1974b). The defect of Merton's traditional norms of science is not that they were wrong but that they failed to take account of their variability within the institution of science.

Finally, the epistemic model ties into the institutional model at a number of points, depending again on what research tradition we bring to bear. From the standpoint of the sociology and the psychology of science, the epistemic model enters by means of the concrete roles required at each phase of scientific inquiry. From the standpoint of the philosophy of science, the epistemic model enters by means of the evaluative criteria necessary to ensure adequate performance at each phase of the inquiry process. Finally, from the standpoint of the history of science, the epistemic structure is related to the evolution of goals, performance criteria, role structure, and control mechanisms over time.

The analytical model of institutions illustrates why the changes we are advocating—greater awareness, appreciation, and cooperation between diverse styles of scientific inquiry—are so difficult to bring about. Such changes call for a simultaneous change in nearly every aspect of the model. We have to change our general concepts of science as embodied not only in its formal goals, roles, and reward structures but in the participants themselves and their individual perspectives; that is, the fact that each of our four methodological types has a very different concept of every aspect of Figure 4. As history bears witness, such intensive changes are not easy to bring about, assuming that we are willing to attempt them or even that such changes are necessary or desirable.

It is not accidental that from their very beginning the social sciences have struggled with the question of method. Method is at the heart of any science. This is especially the case in the social sciences, where the special nature and complexity of its subject matter—human beings—always threaten to overrun both our pretensions to knowledge and our methods of obtaining it. One of the central themes of this book is that if we are ever to achieve an integrated theory of humanity, then our methods can be no less complex than the very phenomenon we are studying; that is, our methods must be as psychologically sophisticated and diverse as humanity itself.

This book is only a beginning. We have only tapped the surface of Jungian psychology in our attempt to analyze science from a Jungian perspective. Much of the psychology we have described has been limited to the more readily apparent and observable properties of the scientific types. We have not examined the deeper, unconscious layers, levels, and properties—for example, the archetypes underlying each type—although in the end it is clear that we are dealing as much with archetypes in regard to science as we are with the realities of different types of scientists (Hillman, 1975b). Given the intensity with which the AS's concept of science has presented itself over the centuries, it is clear that we are dealing with a concept deeply ingrained in the human psyche calling for order, precision, and certainty—rationality in the most Apollonian sense of the term. What is called for in future efforts is an intensive analysis of the mythic images, the archetypes, which support each of the types we have outlined here. We quote from Hillman (1975b, p. 132). "If scientific ideas were connected with their psycho-logical significance, the two realms of objective science and subjective ethics could no longer be so dramatically opposed. By recognizing that a style of thought expresses an archetypal mode of consciousness *including its style of behavior,* the sort of morality to be expected by the psychic premises of scientific theory would belong as corollary to the theory. The idea of science as objective and amoral (or moral only internally, in regard to obeying the requirements of its methods and conventions) has itself an archetypal premise in Apollo, where detachment, dispassion, exclusive masculinity, formal beauty, farsighted aims, elitism are basic fantasies. These have been literalized by science, becoming its belief and behavior." For this reason, the notion of four scientific types must not be taken literally but figuratively as a guide to the psychic consciousness of modern social science.

The notion of a unified science is also an archetypal image (Hillman, 1975b). The desire to bring things together is as much a human need, rooted deep in the human psyche, as is the contrasting need to disunify things, to keep things apart. We do not mean to promote the concept of unification for all times and in all places, nor do we countenance all forms of unification (for example, domination of one of the four types we have discussed at the expense of the others). We are in strong agreement with Diesing that "The widespread attitude that there is only one scientific method, usually one's own, is unfortunate. It produces a distorted view of what other scientists are doing, and as a result blocks much potentially fruitful co-operation on new methods and new theories. My main purpose ... is to argue against a single-method ethnocentrism and to argue that each method is valid in its own way and has its own advantages and disadvantages. Insofar as one form of ethnocentrism is dominant, I wish to argue that social science is not at present, and ought not to be, concerned solely with the experimental-statistical verification of hypothesis and the discovery of general laws" (Diesing, 1971, p. 13). Ultimately we are talking about mutual toleration, appreciation, and even love of the highest sort. We cannot hope to heal humanity if as social scientists we do not start with ourselves. Jung (1971, pp. 333–334) captures the dialectic between separation and unification, between individuality and cooperation, which is the key to a holistic concept of the social sciences:

> The tendency to separate the opposites as much as possible and to strive for singleness of meaning is absolutely necessary for clarity of consciousness, since discrimination is of its essence. But when the separation is carried so far that the complementary opposite is lost sight of, and the blackness of the whiteness, the evil of the good, and the depth of the heights, and so on, is no longer seen, the result is one-sidedness, which is then compensated from the unconsciousness without our help. The counterbalancing is even done against our will, which in consequence must become more and more fanatical until it brings about a catastrophic *enantiodromia.** Wisdom never forgets that all things have two sides, and it would also know how to avoid such calamities if it ever had any power.

*Enantiodromia, from Jung, is defined as "being torn asunder" into pairs of opposites. (See C. G. Jung, *Two Essays on Analytic Psychology*, Princeton University Press, 1953, p. 73.)

References

Ackoff, R. L., and Emery, F. *On Purposeful Systems.* Chicago: Aldine-Atherton, 1972.

Argyris, C. "Some Unintended Consequences of Rigorous Research." *Psychological Bulletin,* 1968, *70,* 185–197.

Argyris, C. *Intervention Theory and Method.* Reading, Mass.: Addison-Wesley, 1973.

Argyris, C., and Schön, D. A. *Theory in Practice: Increasing Professional Effectiveness.* San Francisco: Jossey-Bass, 1974.

Barber, B. *Science and the Social Order.* New York: Collier, 1952.

Barnes, S. B., and Dolby, R. G. A. "The Scientific Ethos: A Deviant Viewpoint." *European Journal of Sociology,* 1970, *11,* 3–25.

Bernard, C. *An Introduction to the Study of Experimental Medicine.* New York: Dover, 1957.

Boguslaw, R. "Values in the Research Society." In E. Glatt and M. W. Shelly (Eds.), *The Research Society.* New York: Gordon and Breach, 1968.

Broverman, I. K., and others. "Sex-Role Stereotypes: A Current Appraisal." *Journal of Social Issues,* 1972, *28,* 59–78.

Campbell, D. T., and Stanley, J. C. *Experimental and Quasi-Experimental Designs for Research.* Chicago: Rand McNally, 1969.

Campbell, N. *What Is Science?* New York: Dover, 1952.

Cassirer, E. *The Philosophy of Symbolic Forms.* Vol. 2: *Mythical Thought.* New Haven, Conn.: Yale University Press, 1955.

Caws, P. "The Structure of Discovery." *Science,* 1969, *166,* 1375–1380.

Churchman, C. W. *Elements of Logic and Formal Science.* Philadelphia: Lippincott, 1940.

Churchman, C. W. *Theory of Experimental Inference.* New York: Macmillan, 1948.

Churchman, C. W. *Prediction and Optimal Decision: Philosophical Issues of a Science of Values.* Englewood Cliffs, N.J.: Prentice-Hall, 1961.

Churchman, C. W. *Challenge to Reason.* New York: McGraw-Hill, 1968.

Churchman, C. W. *The Design of Inquiring Systems.* New York: Basic Books, 1971.

Cole, J. "Patterns of Intellectual Influence in Scientific Research." *Sociology of Education,* 1970, *43,* 377–403.

Cole, S., and Cole, J. "Scientific Output and Recognition: A Study of the Reward System in Science." *American Sociological Review,* 1967, *32,* 377–390.

Cowan, T. A. "Paradoxes of Science Administration." *Science,* 1972, *177,* 964–966.

Cowan, T. A. "Nonrationality in Decision Theory." In C.W. Churchman (Ed.), *Systems and Management Annual.* New York: Petrocelli, 1975.

Crane, D. "The Gatekeepers of Science: Some Factors Affecting the Selection of Articles for Scientific Journals." *The American Sociologist,* 1967, *2,* 195–201.

Crane, D. "Social Structure in a Group of Scientists: A Test of the Invisible College Hypothesis." *American Sociological Review,* 1969, *34,* 335–352.

Crane, D. *Invisible Colleges.* Chicago: University of Chicago Press, 1972.

Cyert, R. M., and MacGrimmon, K. R. "Organization." In L. Sardner and E. Aronson (Eds.), *Handbook of Social Psychology.* Vol. I. Reading, Mass.: Addison-Wesley, 1968.

Davis, M. "That's Interesting! Towards a Phenomenology of Sociology and a Sociology of Phenomenology." *Philosophy of the Social Sciences,* 1971, *4,* 309–344.

Dewey, J. *Essays in Experimental Logic.* New York: Dover, 1953.

Dewey, J. *The Quest for Certainty: A Study of the Relation of Knowledge and Action.* New York: Capricorn, 1960.

Diesing, P. *Reason in Society: Five Types of Decisions and Their Social Conditions.* Urbana: University of Illinois Press, 1962.

Diesing, P. *Patterns of Discovery in the Social Sciences.* Chicago: Aldine-Atherton, 1971.

Duhem, P. *The Aim and Structure of Physical Theory.* Princeton, N.J.: Princeton University Press, 1954.

Eiduson, B. T. *Scientists: Their Psychological World.* New York: Basic Books, 1962.

Eiduson, B. T., and Beckman, L. (Eds.). *Science as a Career Choice.* New York: Russell Sage Foundation, 1973.

Eisenstadt, S. N., and Curelaru, M. *The Form of Sociology— Paradigms and Crises.* New York: Wiley, 1976.

Feigl, H. "The 'Orthodox' View of Theories: Remarks in Defense as Well as Critique." In M. Radner and S. Winokur (Eds.), *Analyses of Theories and Methods of Physics and Psychology.* Minnesota Studies in the Philosophy of Science, Vol. IV. Minneapolis: University of Minnesota Press, 1970.

Feyerabend, P. *Against Method: Outline of an Anarchistic Theory of Knowledge.* London: NLB, 1975.

Freeman, H. *Introduction to Statistical Inference.* Reading, Mass.: Addison-Wesley, 1963.

Friedlander, F. "Behavioral Research as a Transactional Process." *Human Organization,* 1968, *4,* 369–379.

Garvey, W. D. "Scientific Communication: Its Role in the Conduct of Research and Creation of Knowledge." *American Psychologist,* 1971, *26,* 349–362.

Glass, B. "The Ethical Basis of Science." *Science,* 1965, *150,* 1254–1261.

Gordon, G., and others. "A Contingency Model for the Design of Problem-Solving Research Programs: A Perspective on Diffusion Research." *Milbank Memorial Fund Quarterly,* Spring 1974, pp. 185–220.

Gulick, L., and Urwick, L. F. (Eds.). *Papers on the Science of Public Administration.* Clifton, N.J.: Augustus M. Kelley, 1969. (Originally published in 1937.)

Haack, S. *Deviant Logic: Some Philosophical Issues.* Cambridge, England: Cambridge University Press, 1974.

Hagstrom, W. *The Scientific Community.* New York: Basic Books, 1965.

Hanson, N. R. *Patterns of Discovery.* Cambridge, England: University of Cambridge Press, 1965.

Hanson, N. R. *Perception and Discovery.* San Francisco: W. H. Freeman, 1969.

Hanson, N. R. "A Picture Theory of Meaning." In M. Radner and S. Winokur (Eds.), *Analyses of Theories and Methods of Physics and Psychology.* Minnesota Studies in the Philosophy of Science, Vol. IV. Minneapolis: University of Minnesota Press, 1970.

Harré, R., and Secord, P. *The Explanation of Social Behavior.* Totowa, N.J.: Littlefield Adams, 1973.

Heap, J. L., and Roth, P. A. "On Phenomenological Sociology." *American Sociological Review,* 1973, *38,* 354–367.

Helfrich, M. L. *The Social Role of the Executive's Wife.* Columbus: Bureau of Business Research, Ohio State University, 1965.

Hempel, C. G. *Aspects of Scientific Explanation.* New York: Free Press, 1965.

Hempel, C. G. "On The 'Standard Conception' of Scientific Theories." In M. Radner and S. Winokur (Eds.), *Analyses of Theories and Methods of Physics and Psychology.* Minnesota Studies in the Philosophy of Science, Vol. IV. Minneapolis: University of Minnesota Press, 1970.

Hensler, D. "Perceptions of the National Science Foundation Peer Review Process: A Report on a Survey of NSF Reviewers and Principal Investigators." Paper prepared for the committee on Peer Review, National Science Board, Washington, D.C., September 1976.

Hesse, M. B. *Models and Analogies in Science.* Notre Dame, Ind.: University of Notre Dame Press, 1966.

Hillman, J. "The Fiction of Case History: A Round." In J. B. Wiggins (Eds.), *Religion as Story.* New York: Harper & Row, 1975a.

Hillman, J. *Revisioning Psychology.* New York: Harper & Row, 1975b.

Holton, G. *Thematic Origins of Scientific Thought, Kepler to Einstein.* Cambridge: Harvard University Press, 1973.

Holton, G. "On Being Caught Between Dionysians and Apollonians." In G. Holton (Ed.), *Science and Its Public: The Changing Relationship.* Boston: Daedalus, 1974.

Hudson, L. *Contrary Imaginations*. New York: Schocken Books, 1966.

Jourard, S. M. *Disclosing Man to Himself*. New York: D. Van Nostrand, 1968.

Jung, C. G. *Mysterium Conjunctionis: An Inquiry into the Separation and Synthesis of Psychic Opposites in Alchemy*. (R. F. C. Hull, Trans.) Princeton, N.J.: Princeton University Press, 1963.

Jung, C. G. *Analytical Psychology, Its Theory and Practice*. New York: Pantheon, 1968.

Jung, C. G. *Collected Works*. (R. F. C. Hull, Rev. trans.) Vol. 6: *Psychological Types*. Princeton, N.J.: Princeton University Press, 1971.

Kant, I. *Critique of Practical Reason*. (L. W. Beck, Trans.) Indianapolis: Bobbs-Merrill, 1956. (Originally published 1788.)

Kant, I. *Critique of Pure Reason*. (N. K. Smith, Trans.) London: Macmillan, 1958. (Originally published 1781.)

Kanter, R. M. *Men and Women of the Corporation*. New York: Basic Books, 1977.

Kilmann, R. H., and Mitroff, I. I. "Defining Real-World Problems: A Social Science Approach." Unpublished manuscript, 1977, available from R. H. Kilmann, Graduate School of Business, University of Pittsburgh.

King, M. D. "Reason, Tradition, and the Progressiveness of Science." *History and Theory: Studies in the Philosophy of History*, 1971, *10*, 3–32.

Kosok, M. "The Formalization of Hegel's Dialectical Logic." In A. MacIntyre (Ed.), *Hegel, a Collection of Critical Essays*. New York: Doubleday, 1972.

Kubie, L. "Some Unsolved Problems of the Scientific Career." *American Scientist*, 1953, *41*, 596–613; and 1954, *42*, 104–112.

Kubie, L. *Neurotic Distortion of the Creative Process*. Lawrence: University of Kansas Press, 1961.

Kuhn, T. S. *The Structure of Scientific Revolutions*. Chicago: University of Chicago Press, 1962.

Lakatos, I. "Falsification and the Methodology of Scientific Research Programmes." In I. Lakatos and A. Musgrave (Eds.), *Criticism and the Growth of Knowledge*. Cambridge, England: Cambridge University Press, 1970.

Lakatos, I., and Musgrave, A. (Eds.). *Criticism and the Growth of Knowledge.* Cambridge, England: Cambridge University Press, 1970.

Laudan, L. "On the Impossibility of Crucial Falsifying Experiments." *Philosophy of Science,* 1965, *32,* 39–68.

Leach, E. "Anthropological Aspects of Language: Animal Categories and Verbal Abuse." In P. Maranda (Ed.), *Mythology.* Middlesex, England: Penguin Books, 1973.

Levine, M. "Scientific Method and the Adversary Model: Some Preliminary Thoughts." *American Psychologist,* September 1974, pp. 661–677.

Lodahl, J. B., and Gordon, G. "The Structure of Scientific Fields and the Functioning of University Graduate Departments." *American Sociological Review,* 1972, *37,* 57–72.

McClelland, D. C. "On the Dynamics of Creative Physical Scientists." In L. Hudson (Ed.), *The Ecology of Human Intelligence.* Middlesex, England: Penguin Books, 1970.

McGuire, W. J. "The Yin and Yang of Progress in Social Psychology: Seven Koan." *Journal of Personality and Social Psychology,* 1973, *26,* 446–456.

Mahoney, M. *Scientist as Subject: The Psychological Imperative.* Cambridge, Mass.: Balinger, 1976.

Manuel, F. E. *A Portrait of Isaac Newton,* Cambridge, Mass.: Harvard University Press, 1968.

Maslow, A. H. *The Psychology of Science.* New York: Harper & Row, 1966.

Mason, R. O. "A Dialectical Approach to Strategic Planning." *Management Science,* 1969, *15,* B-403–B-414.

Maurer, J. G. (Ed.). *Readings in Organization Theory: Open Systems Approaches.* New York: Random House, 1971.

Maxwell, N. "A Critique of Popper's Views on Scientific Method." *Philosophy of Science,* 1972, *39,* 131–152.

Merton, R. K. "The Ambivalence of Scientists." *Bulletin of the Johns Hopkins Hospital,* 1938, *112,* 115–126.

Merton, R. K. "Science and Technology in a Democratic Order." *Journal of Legal and Political Sociology,* 1942, *1,* 115–126.

Merton, R. K. "Priorities in Scientific Discovery." *American Sociological Review,* 1957, *22,* 635–659.

Merton, R. K. "Singletons and Multiples in Scientific Discovery: A Chapter in the Sociology of Science." *Proceedings of the American Philosophical Society*, 1961, *105*, 470–486.

Merton, R. K. "The Ambivalence of Scientists." *Bulletin of the Johns Hopkins Hospital*, February 1963, *112*, 77–97.

Merton, R. K. *Social Theory and Social Structure*. New York: Free Press, 1968.

Merton, R. K. "Behavior Patterns of Scientists." *American Scientist*, 1969, *57*, 1–23.

Merton, R. K. "Structural Analysis in Sociology." In P. M. Blau (Ed.), *Approaches to the Study of Social Structure*. New York: Free Press, 1975.

Merton, R. K., and Zuckerman, H. "Age, Aging, and Age Structure." In R. K. Merton (Ed.), *The Sociology of Science*. Chicago: University of Chicago Press, 1973.

Mill, J. S. *A System of Logic*. (8th ed.) New York: Longmans, Green, 1872.

Mitroff, I. I. "Norms and Counter-Norms in a Select Group of the Apollo Moon Scientists: A Case Study of the Ambivalence of Scientists." *American Sociological Review*, 1974a, *39*, 579–595.

Mitroff, I. I. *The Subjective Side of Science: An Inquiry into the Psychology of the Apollo Moon Scientists*. Amsterdam, The Netherlands: Elsevier, 1974b.

Mitroff, I. I. "Towards a Theory of Systemic Problem Solving." *International Journal of General Systems*, 1977, *4*.

Mitroff, I. I., and Chubin, D. E. "Peer Review: A Dialectical Policy Analysis." Unpublished manuscript, 1978, available from I. I. Mitroff, Graduate School of Business, University of Pittsburgh.

Mitroff, I. I., and Emshoff, J. "On Strategic Assumption Making: A Dialectical Approach to Policy Analysis and Evaluation." *Academy of Management Review*, forthcoming.

Mitroff, I. I., and Featheringham, T. "Towards a Behavioral Theory of Systemic Hypothesis-Testing and the Error of the Third Kind." *Theory and Decision*, 1976, *7*, 205–220.

Mitroff, I. I., Jacob, T., and Moore, E. T. "On the Shoulders of the Spouses of Scientists." *Social Studies of Science*, 1977, *7*, 303–327.

Mitroff, I. I., and Kilmann, R. H. "On Organizational Stories: An Approach to the Design and Analysis of Organizations Through Myths and Stories." In R. Kilmann, L. Pondy, and D. Slevin

(Eds.), *The Management of Organization Design.* Amsterdam, The Netherlands: North Holland, 1976.

Mitroff, I. I., and Turoff, M. "On Measuring the Conceptual Errors in Large Scale Social Experiments: The Future as Decision." *Journal of Technological Forecasting and Social Change,* 1974, *6,* 389–402.

Mitroff, I. I., and others. "On Managing Science in the Systems Age: Two Schemas for the Study of Science as a Whole Systems Phenomenon." *Interfaces,* 1974, *4,* 46–58.

Morse, E. V., and Gordon, G. "Cognitive Skills: A Determinant of Scientists' Local-Cosmopolital Orientation." *Academy of Management Journal,* 1974, *17,* 709–723.

Mulkay, M. J. "Some Aspects of Cultural Growth in the Natural Sciences." *Social Research,* 1969, *39,* 22–53.

Mulkay, M. J. "Conformity and Innovation in Science." *Sociological Review Monograph,* 1972, *18,* 5–24.

Mullins, N. C. "The Development of a Scientific Specialty: The Phage Group and the Origins of Molecular Biology." *Minerva,* 1972, *10,* 51–82.

Mullins, N. C. "The Development of Specialties in Social Science: The Case of Ethnomethodology." *Science Studies,* 1973, *3.*

Myers-Briggs, I. *Manual for the Myers-Briggs Type Indicator.* Princeton, N.J.: Educational Testing Service, 1962.

Nagel, E. *The Structure of Science: Problems in the Logic of Scientific Explanation.* New York: Harcourt Brace Jovanovich, 1961.

Pascal, B. *Pensées.* New York: Dutton, 1958.

Pepper, S. C. *World Hypotheses.* Berkeley: University of California Press, 1942.

Phillips, D. "Epistemology and the Sociology of Knowledge: The Contributions of Mannheim, Mills, and Merton." *Theory and Society,* 1974, *1,* 59–88.

Polanyi, M. *Personal Knowledge.* New York: Harper & Row, 1958.

Popper, K. R. *The Logic of Scientific Discovery.* New York: Harper & Row, 1965.

Popper, K. R. "Normal Science and Its Dangers." In I. Lakatos and A. Musgrave (Eds.), *Criticism and the Growth of Knowledge.* Cambridge, England: University of Cambridge Press, 1970.

Price, D. J. de Solla. *Little Science, Big Science.* New York: Columbia University Press, 1963.

Price, D. J. de Solla. "Networks of Scientific Papers." *Science,* 1969, *149,* 510–515.

Quine, W. V. O. "Two Dogmas of Empiricism." In *From a Logical Point of View.* New York: Harper & Row, 1953.

Quine, W. V. O. "Carnap and Logical Truth." *Synthese,* 1960, *18.*

Quine, W. V. O. *Philosophy of Logic.* Englewood Cliffs, N.J.: Prentice-Hall, 1970.

Quinn, P. "The Status of the D-Thesis." *Philosophy of Science,* 1969, *4,* 381–399.

Radnitzky, G. "Ways of Looking at Science: A Synoptic Study of Contemporary Schools of 'Metascience.'" *General Systems,* 1969, *14,* 187–191.

Ravetz, J. R. *Scientific Knowledge and Its Social Problems.* Oxford, England: Clarendon Press, 1971.

Reichenbach, H. *Experience and Prediction: An Analysis of the Foundation and the Structure of Knowledge.* Berkeley: University of California Press, 1968.

Ritzer, G. *Sociology: A Multiple Paradigm Science.* Boston: Allyn & Bacon, 1975.

Roe, A. "A Psychological Study of Eminent Physical Scientists." *Genetic Psychology Monographs,* 1951, *43,* 121–135.

Roe, A. *The Making of a Scientist.* New York: Dodd, Mead, 1953.

Roe, A. "A Psychological Study of Eminent Psychologists and Anthropologists and a Comparison with Biological and Physical Scientists." *Psychological Monographs,* 1954, *67.*

Roe, A. "The Psychology of the Scientist." *Science,* 1961, *134,* 456–459.

Rossi, P. H. "Testing for Success and Failure in Social Action." In P. H. Rossi and W. Williams (Eds.), *Evaluating Social Programs.* New York: Seminar Press, 1972.

Roszak, T. *Where the Wasteland Ends: Politics and Transcendance in Postindustrial Society.* New York: Doubleday, 1973.

Rowan, J. "The New Paradigm in Research." Unpublished paper, June, 1976a.

Rowan, J. *Ordinary Ecstasy: Humanistic Psychology in Action.* London: Routledge & Kegan Paul, 1976b.

Sarton, G. *The History of Science and the New Humanism.* Bloomington: Indiana University Press, 1962.

Scheffler, I. *Science and Subjectivity.* Indianapolis: Bobbs-Merrill, 1967.

Scheffler, I. "Discussion: Vision and Revolution: A Postscript on Kuhn." *Philosophy of Science,* 1972, *39,* 366–374.

Simon, H. A. "Does Scientific Discovery Have a Logic?" *Philosophy of Science,* 1973, *40,* 471–480.

Storer, N. W. *The Social System of Science.* New York: Holt, Rinehart and Winston, 1966.

Szent-Gyorgyi, A. "Dionysians and Apollonians." Letter to *Science,* 1972, *176* (4038), 966.

Tart, C. T. "States of Consciousness and State Specific Sciences." *Science,* 1972, *176,* 1203–1210.

Thomas, K. W., and Kilmann, R. H. *Thomas-Kilmann Conflict Mode Instrument.* New York: Xicom, 1974.

Torbert, W. R. *Creating a Community of Inquiry: Conflict, Collaboration, Transformation.* New York: Wiley, 1976.

Toulmin, S. *Human Understanding.* Vol. I. Princeton, N.J.: Princeton University Press, 1972.

U.S. Congress, House Committee on Science and Technology, Subcommittee on Science, Research, and Technology. *National Science Foundation Peer Review.* Vol. I. 94th Cong., 2d sess., January 1976.

Weber, M. *The Theory of Social and Economic Organization.* New York: Free Press, 1947.

Wedeking, G. "Duhem, Quinn, and Grünbaum on Falsification." *Philosophy of Science,* 1969, *36,* 375–380.

Westfall, R. S. "Newton and the Fudge Factor." *Science,* 1973, *179,* 751–756.

Whyte, W. F. *Street Corner Society.* Chicago: University of Chicago Press, 1943.

Wolf, R. "Contradictions and the Logical Systems." Paper presented at Conference on Dialectical Logic, Glendon College, Toronto, Canada, August 1975.

Ziman, J. *Public Knowledge: an Essay Concerning the Social Dimension of Science.* New York: Cambridge University Press, 1968.

Zuckerman, H. "Nobel Laureates in Science." *American Sociological Review,* 1967, *32,* 391–403.

Zuckerman, H. "Stratification in American Science." *Sociological Enquiry,* 1970, *40,* 235–257.

Index

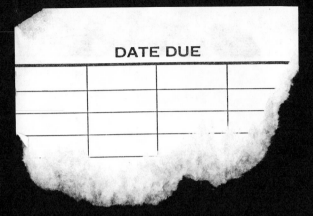

DATE DUE